SPHERICAL TRIGONOMETRY

SPHERICAL TRIGONOMETRY

Fifth Edition

For the Use of Colleges and Schools.

With Numerous Examples.

I. Todhunter, M.A., F.R.S.,

Honorary Fellow of St John's College,

Cambridge.

MJP PUBLISHERS

Reprint of 1886 Edition
MJP first reprint : 2008

ISBN 81-8094-052-7   **MJP PUBLISHERS**
© Publishers, 2008   47, Nallathambi Street
All rights reserved   Triplicane
Printed and bound in India   Chennai 600 005

MJP 046

PREFACE

The present work is constructed on the same plan as my treatise on Plane Trigonometry, to which it is intended as a sequel; it contains all the propositions usually included under the head of Spherical Trigonometry, together with a large collection of examples for exercise. In the course of the work reference is made to preceding writers from whom assistance has been obtained; besides these writers I have consulted the treatises on Trigonometry by Lardner, Lefebure de Fourcy, and Snowball, and the treatise on Geometry published in the Library of Useful Knowledge. The examples have been chiefly selected from the University and College Examination Papers.

In the account of Napier's Rules of Circular Parts an explanation has been given of a method of proof devised by Napier, which seems to have been overlooked by most modern writers on the subject. I have had the advantage of access to an unprinted Memoir on this point by the late R. L. Ellis of Trinity College; Mr Ellis had in fact rediscovered for himself Napier's own method. For the use of this Memoir and for some valuable references on the subject I am indebted to the Dean of Ely.

Considerable labour has been bestowed on the text in order to render it comprehensive and accurate, and the examples have all been carefully verified; and thus I venture to hope that the work will be found useful by Students and Teachers.

I. TODHUNTER
St John's College,
August 15, 1859

CONTENTS

GREAT AND SMALL CIRCLES

1. A SPHERE is a solid bounded by a surface every point of which is equally distant from a fixed point which is called the *centre* of the sphere. The straight line which joins any point of the surface with the centre is called a *radius*. A straight line drawn through the centre and terminated both ways by the surface is called a *diameter*.

2. *The section of the surface of a sphere made by any plane is a circle.*

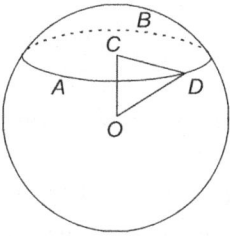

Let *AB* be the section of the surface of a sphere made by any plane, *O* the centre of the sphere. Draw *OC* perpendicular to the plane; take any point *D* in the section and join *OD*, *CD*.

Since OC is perpendicular to the plane, the angle OCD is a right angle; therefore $CD = \sqrt{(OD^2 - OC^2)}$. Now O and C are fixed points, so that OC is constant; and OD is constant, being the radius of the sphere; hence CD is constant. Thus all points in the plane section are equally distant from the fixed point C; therefore the section is a circle of which C is the centre.

3. The section of the surface of a sphere by a plane is called a *great circle* if the plane passes through the centre of the sphere, and a *small circle* if the plane does not pass through the centre of the sphere. Thus the radius of a great circle is equal to the radius of the sphere.

4. Through the centre of a sphere and any two points on the surface a plane can be drawn; and only one plane can be drawn, except when the two points are the extremities of a diameter of the sphere, and then an infinite number of such planes can be drawn. Hence only one great circle can be drawn through two given points on the surface of a sphere, except when the points are the extremities of a diameter of the sphere. When only one great circle can be drawn through two given points, the great circle is unequally divided at the two points; we shall for brevity speak of the shorter of the two arcs as *the* arc of a great circle joining the two points.

5. The *axis* of any circle of a sphere is that diameter of the sphere which is perpendicular to the plane of the circle; the extremities of the axis are called the *poles* of the circle. The poles of a great circle are equally distant from the plane of the circle. The poles of a small circle are not equally distant from the

plane of the circle; they may be called respectively the *nearer* and *further* pole; sometimes the nearer pole is for brevity called *the* pole.

6. *A pole of a circle is equally distant from every point of the circumference of the circle.*

Let O be the centre of the sphere, AB any circle of the sphere, C the centre of the circle, P and P' the poles of the circle. Take any point D in the circumference of the circle; join CD, OD, PD. Then $PD = \sqrt{(PC^2 + CD^2)}$; and PC and CD are constant, therefore PD is constant. Suppose a great circle to pass through the points P and D; then the chord PD is constant, and therefore the arc of a great circle intercepted between P and D is constant for all positions of D on the circle AB.

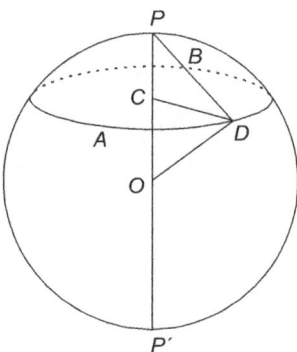

Thus the distance of a pole of a circle from every point of the circumference of the circle is constant, whether that distance be measured by the straight line joining the points, or by the arc of a great circle intercepted between the points.

7. *The arc of a great circle which is drawn from a pole of a great circle to any point in its circumference is a quadrant.*

Let *P* be a pole of the great circle *ABC*; then the arc *PA* is a quadrant.

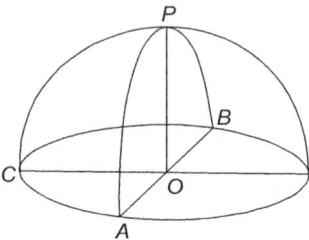

For let *O* be the centre of the sphere, and draw *PO*. Then *PO* is at right angles to the plane *ABC*, because *P* is the pole of *ABC*, therefore *POA* is a right angle, and the arc *PA* is a quadrant.

8. *The angle subtended at the centre of a sphere by the arc of a great circle which joins the poles of two great circles is equal to the inclination of the planes of the great circles.*

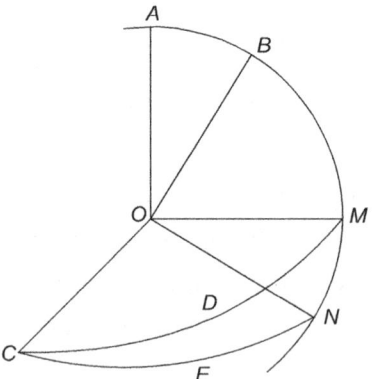

Let O be the centre of the sphere, CD, CE the great circles intersecting at C, A and B the poles of CD and CE respectively.

Draw a great circle through A and B, meeting CD and CE at M and N respectively. Then AO is perpendicular to OC, which is a straight line in the plane OCD; and BO is perpendicular to OC, which is a straight line in the plane OCE; therefore OC is perpendicular to the plane AOB (Euclid, xi. 4); and therefore OC is perpendicular to the straight lines OM and ON, which are in the plane AOB. Hence MON is the angle of inclination of the planes OCD and OCE. And the angle

$$AOB = AOM - BOM = BON - BOM = MON.$$

9. By the angle between two great circles is meant *the angle of inclination of the planes of the circles*. Thus, in the figure of the preceding Article, the angle between the great circles CD and CE is the angle MON.

In the figure to Art. 6, since PO is perpendicular to the plane ACB, every plane which contains PO is at right angles to the plane ACB. Hence the angle between the plane of any circle and the plane of a great circle which passes through its poles is a right angle.

10. *Two great circles bisect each other*.

For since the plane of each great circle passes through the centre of the sphere, the line of intersection of these planes is a diameter of the sphere, and therefore also a diameter of each great circle; therefore the great circles are bisected at the points where they meet.

11. *If the arcs of great circles joining a point P on the surface of a sphere with two other points A and C on the surface of the sphere, which are not at opposite extremities of a diameter, be each of them equal to a quadrant, P is a pole of the great circle through A and C.* (See the figure of Art. 7.)

For suppose *PA* and *PC* to be quadrants, and *O* the centre of the sphere; then since *PA* and *PC* are quadrants, the angles *P OC* and *POA* are right angles. Hence *PO* is at right angles to the plane *AOC*, and *P* is a pole of the great circle *AC*.

12. Great circles which pass through the poles of a great circle are called *secondaries* to that circle. Thus, in the figure of Art. 8 the point *C* is a pole of *ABMN*, and therefore *CM* and *CN* are parts of secondaries to *ABMN*. And the angle between *CM* and *CN* is measured by *MN*; that is, *the angle between any two great circles is measured by the arc they intercept on the great circle to which they are secondaries*.

13. *If from a point on the surface of a sphere there can be drawn two arcs of great circles, not parts of the same great circle, the planes of which are at right angles to the plane of a given circle, that point is a pole of the given circle.*

For, since the planes of these arcs are at right angles to the plane of the given circle, the line in which they intersect is perpendicular to the plane of the given circle, and is therefore the axis of the given circle; hence the point from which the arcs are drawn is a pole of the circle.

14. *To compare the arc of a small circle subtending any angle at the centre of the circle with the arc of a great circle subtending the same angle at its centre.*

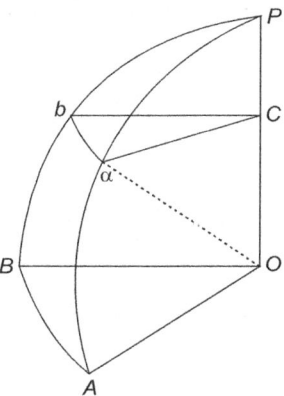

Let *ab* be the arc of a small circle, *C* the centre of the circle, *P* the pole of the circle, *O* the centre of the sphere. Through *P* draw the great circles *P aA* and *PbB*, meeting the great circle of which *P* is a pole, at *A* and *B* respectively; draw *Ca*, *Cb*, *OA*, *OB*. Then *Ca*, *Cb*, *OA*, *OB* are all perpendicular to *OP*; because the planes *aCb* and *AOB* are perpendicular to *OP* ; therefore *Ca* is parallel to *OA*, and *Cb* is parallel to OB. Therefore the angle *aCb* = the angle *AOB* (Euclid, xi. 10).

Hence,

$$\frac{arc\,ab}{\text{radius}\,Ca} = \frac{arc\,AB}{\text{radius}\,OA}, (Plane\,Trigonometry, \text{Art.}18);$$

therefore,

$$\frac{arc\,ab}{arc\,AB} = \frac{Ca}{OA} = \frac{Ca}{Oa} = \sin POa.$$

2

SPHERICAL TRIANGLES

15. Spherical Trigonometry investigates the relations which subsist between the angles of the plane faces which form a solid angle and the angles at which the plane faces are inclined to each other.

16. Suppose that the angular point of a solid angle is made the centre of a sphere; then the planes which form the solid angle will cut the sphere in arcs of great circles. Thus a figure will be formed on the surface of the sphere which is called a *spherical triangle* if it is bounded by *three* arcs of great circles; this will be the case when the solid angle is formed by the meeting of *three* plane angles. If the solid angle be formed by the meeting of *more than three* plane angles, the corresponding figure on the surface of the sphere is bounded by more than three arcs of great circles, and is called a *spherical polygon.*

17. The three arcs of great circles which form a spherical triangle are called the *sides* of the spherical triangle; the angles formed by the arcs at the points where they meet are called the *angles* of the spherical triangle. (See Art. 9.)

18. Thus, let O be the centre of a sphere, and suppose a solid angle formed at O by the meeting of three plane angles. Let AB, BC, CA be the arcs of great circles in which the planes cut the sphere; then ABC is a spherical triangle, and the arcs AB, BC, CA are its sides.

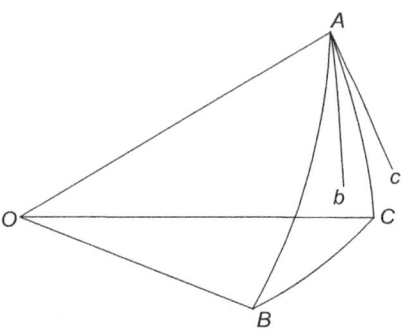

Suppose Ab the tangent at A to the arc AB, and Ac the tangent at A to the arc AC, the tangents being drawn from A *towards* B and C respectively; then the angle bAc is one of the angles of the spherical triangle. Similarly angles formed in like manner at B and C are the other angles of the spherical triangle.

19. The principal part of a treatise on Spherical Trigonometry consists of theorems relating to spherical triangles; it is therefore necessary to obtain an accurate conception of a spherical triangle and its parts.

It will be seen that what are called *sides* of a spherical triangle are really *arcs* of great circles, and these arcs are proportional to the three plane angles which form the solid angle corresponding to the spherical triangle. Thus, in the figure of the preceding Article, the arc AB forms one side of the spherical triangle *ABC*, and the plane angle *AOB* is measured by the fraction $\dfrac{\text{arc } AB}{\text{radius } OA}$; and thus the arc *AB* is proportional to the angle *AOB* so long as we keep to the same sphere.

The *angles* of a spherical triangle are the inclinations of the plane faces which form the solid angle; for since *Ab* and *Ac* are both perpendicular to *OA*, the angle *bAc* is the angle of inclination of the planes *OAB* and *OAC*.

20. The letters *A*, *B*, *C* are generally used to denote the *angles* of a spherical triangle, and the letters *a*, *b*, *c* are used to denote the *sides*. As in the case of plane triangles, *A*, *B*, and *C* may be used to denote the numerical values of the angles expressed in *terms of any unit*, provided we understand distinctly what the unit is. Thus, if the angle *C* be a right angle, we may say that $C = 90°$, or that $C = \dfrac{\pi}{2}$, according as we adopt for the unit a degree or the angle subtended at the centre by an arc equal to the radius. So also, as the sides of a spherical triangle are proportional to the angles subtended at the centre of the sphere, we may use *a*, *b*, *c* to denote the numerical values of those angles in terms of any unit. We shall usually suppose both the angles and sides of a spherical triangle expressed in *circular measure.*(*Plane Trigonometry*, Art. 20.)

21. In future, unless the contrary be distinctly stated, any arc drawn on the surface of a sphere will be supposed to be an arc of a *great* circle.

22. In spherical triangles each side is restricted to be less than a semicircle; this is of course a *convention*, and it is adopted because it is found convenient.

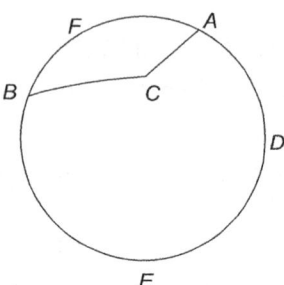

Thus, in the figure, the arc *ADEB* is greater than a semicircumference, and we might, if we pleased, consider *ADEB*, *AC*, and *BC* as forming a triangle, having its angular points at *A*, *B*, and *C*. But we agree to exclude such triangles from our consideration; and the triangle having its angular points at *A*, *B*, and *C*, will be understood to be that formed by *AFB*, *BC*, and *CA*.

23. From the restriction of the preceding Article it will follow that *any angle of a spherical triangle is less than two right angles.*

For suppose a triangle formed by *BC*, *CA*, and *BEDA*, having the angle *BCA* greater than two right angles. Then suppose *D* to denote the point at which the arc *BC*, if produced, will meet *AE*; then *BED* is a semicircle by Art. 10, and therefore *BEA* is greater than a semicircle; thus the proposed triangle is not one of those which we consider.

SPHERICAL GEOMETRY

24. The relations between the sides and angles of a Spherical Triangle, which are investigated in treatises on Spherical Trigonometry, are chiefly such as involve the *Trigonometrical Functions* of the sides and angles. Before proceeding to these, however, we shall collect, under the head of Spherical Geometry, some theorems which involve the sides and angles *themselves*, and not their trigonometrical ratios.

25. *Polar triangle.* Let *ABC* be any spherical triangle, and let the points *A'*, *B'*, *C'* be those poles of the arcs *BC*, *CA*, *AB* respectively which lie on the same sides of them as the opposite angles *A*, *B*, *C*; then the triangle *A'B'C'* is said to be the *polar triangle* of the triangle *ABC*.

Since there are two poles for each side of a spherical triangle, *eight* triangles can be formed having for their angular points poles of the sides of the given triangle; but there is only one triangle in which these poles *A'*, *B'*, *C'* lie towards the same parts with the corresponding angles *A, B, C*; and this is the triangle which is known under the name of the *polar triangle*.

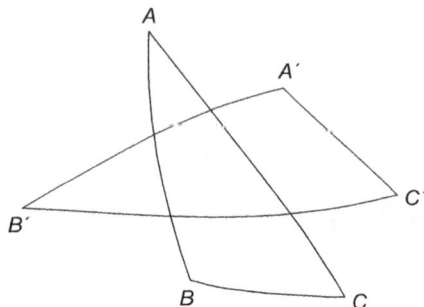

The triangle *ABC* is called the *primitive* triangle with respect to the triangle *A'B'C'*.

26. *If one triangle be the polar triangle of another, the latter will be the polar triangle of the former.*

Let *ABC* be any triangle, *A'B'C'* the polar triangle: then *ABC* will be the polar triangle of *A'B'C'*.

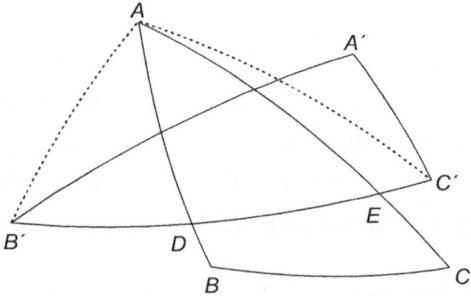

For since *B'* is a pole of *AC*, the arc *AB'* is a quadrant, and since *C'* is a pole of *BA*, the arc *AC'* is a quadrant (Art. 7); therefore *A* is a pole of *B'C*. (Art. 11). Also *A* and *A'* are on the same side of $B'C'$; for A and A' are by hypothesis on the same side of BC, therefore $A'A$ is less than a quadrant; and since A is a pole of $B'C'$, and AA is less than a quadrant, A and A' are on the same side of $B'C'$.

Similarly it may be shewn that B is a pole of $C'A'$, and that B and B' are on the same side of $C'A'$; also that C is a pole of $A'B'$, and that C and C' are on the same side of $A'B'$. Thus ABC is the polar triangle of $A'B'C'$.

27. *The sides and angles of the polar triangle are respectively the supplements of the angles and sides of the primitive triangle.*

For let the arc $B'C'$, produced if necessary, meet the arcs AB, AC, produced if necessary, at the points D and E respectively; then since A is a pole of $B'C'$, the spherical angle A is measured by the arc DE (Art. 12). But $B'E$ and $C'D$ are each quadrants; therefore DE and $B'C'$ are together equal to a semicircle; that is, the angle subtended by $B'C'$ at the centre of the sphere is the supplement of the angle A. This we may express for shortness thus; $B'C'$ is the supplement of A. Similarly it may be shown that $C'A'$ is the supplement of B, and $A'B'$ the supplement of C.

And since ABC is the polar triangle of $A'B'C'$, it follows that BC, CA, AB are respectively the supplements of A', B', C'; that is, A', B', C' are respectively the supplements of BC, CA, AB.

From these properties a primitive triangle and its polar triangle are sometimes called *supplemental triangles*.

Thus, if A, B, C, a, b, c denote respectively the angles and the sides of a spherical triangle, all expressed in circular measure, and A', B', C', a', b', c' those of the polar triangle, we have

$$A' = \pi - a, \quad B = \pi - b, \quad C' = \pi - c,$$
$$a' = \pi - A, \quad b' = \pi - B, \quad c' = \pi - C.$$

28. The preceding result is of great importance; for if any general theorem be demonstrated with respect to the sides and the angles of any spherical triangle it holds of course for the polar triangle also. *Thus any such theorem will remain true when the angles are changed into the supplements of the corresponding sides and the sides into the supplements of the corresponding angles.* We shall see several examples of this principle in the next Chapter.

29. *Any two sides of a spherical triangle are together greater than the third side.* (See the figure of Art. 18.)

For any two of the three plane angles which form the solid angle at O are together greater than the third (Euclid, xi. 20). Therefore any two of the arcs AB, BC, CA, are together greater than the third.

From this proposition it is obvious that any side of a spherical triangle is greater than the difference of the other two.

30. *The sum of the three sides of a spherical triangle is less than the circumference of a great circle.* (See the figure of Art. 18.)

For the sum of the three plane angles which form the solid angle at O is less than four right angles (Euclid, XI. 21); therefore

$$\frac{AB}{OA} + \frac{BC}{OA} + \frac{CA}{OA} \text{ is less than } 2\pi,$$

therefore, $AB + BC + CD$ is less than $2\pi \times OA$;

that is, the sum of the arcs is less than the circumference of a great circle.

31. The propositions contained in the preceding two Articles may be extended. Thus, if there be any polygon which has each of its angles less than two right angles, *any one side is less than the sum of all the others*. This may be proved by repeated use of Art. 29. Suppose, for example, that the figure has four sides, and let the angular points be denoted by A, B, C, D.

Then

$$AD + BC \text{ is greater than } AC;$$

therefore, $AB + BC + CD$ is greater than $AC + CD$, and *a fortiori* greater than AD.

Again, if there be any polygon which has each of its angles less than two right angles, *the sum of its sides will be less than the circumference of a great circle*. This follows from Euclid, XI. 21, in the manner shewn in Art. 30.

32. *The three angles of a spherical triangle are together greater than two right angles and less than six right angles.*

Let A, B, C be the *angles* of a spherical triangle; let a', b', c' be the *sides* of the polar triangle. Then by Art. 30,

$$a' + b' + c' \text{ is less than } 2\pi,$$

that is, $\pi - A + \pi - B + \pi - C$ is less than 2π;

therefore, $A + B + C$ is greater than.

And since each of the angles A, B, C is less than π, the sum $A + B + C$ is less than 3π.

33. *The angles at the base of an isosceles spherical triangle are equal.*

Let ABC be a spherical triangle having $AC = BC$; let O be the centre of the sphere. Draw tangents at the points A and B to the arcs AC and BC respectively; these will meet OC produced at the same point S, and AS will be equal to BS.

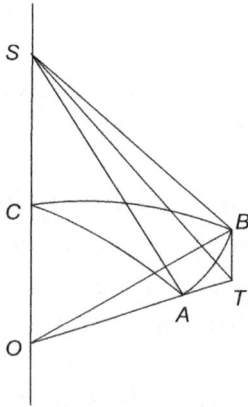

Draw tangents *AT* , *BT* at the points *A*, *B* to the arc *AB*; then *AT* = *TB*; join *TS*. In the two triangles *SAT*, *SBT* the sides *SA*, *AT*, *TS* are equal to *SB*, *BT*, *TS* respectively; therefore the angle *SAT* is equal to the angle *SBT* ; and these are the angles at the base of the spherical triangle.

The figure supposes *AC* and *BC* to be less than quadrants; if they are greater than quadrants the tangents to *AC* and *BC* will meet on *CO* produced through *O* instead of through *C*, and the demonstration may be completed as before. If *AC* and *BC* are quadrants, the angles at the base are right angles by Arts. 11 and 9.

34. *If two angles of a spherical triangle are equal, the opposite sides are equal.*

Since the primitive triangle has two equal angles, the polar triangle has two equal sides; therefore in the polar triangle the angles opposite the equal sides are equal by Art. 33. Hence in the primitive triangle the sides opposite the equal angles are equal.

35. *If one angle of a spherical triangle be greater than another, the side opposite the greater angle is greater than the side opposite the less angle.*

Let *ABC* be a spherical triangle, and let the angle *ABC* be greater than the angle *BAC*: then the side *AC* will be greater than the side *BC*. At *B* make the angle *ABD* equal to the angle *BAD*; then *BD* is equal to *AD* (Art. 34), and *BD* + *DC* is greater than *BC* (Art. 29); therefore *AD* + *DC* is greater than *BC*; that is, *AC* is greater than *BC*.

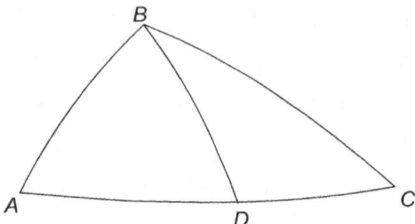

36. *If one side of a spherical triangle be greater than another, the angle opposite the greater side is greater than the angle opposite the less side.*

This follows from the preceding Article by means of the polar triangle.

Or thus; suppose the side *AC* greater than the side *BC*, then the angle *ABC* will be greater than the angle *BAC*. For the angle *ABC* cannot be less than the angle *BAC* by Art. 35, and the angle *ABC* cannot be equal to the angle *BAC* by Art. 34; therefore the angle *ABC* must be greater than the angle *BAC*.

This Chapter might be extended; but it is unnecessary to do so because the Trigonometrical formulæ of the next Chapter supply an easy method of investigating the theorems of Spherical Geometry. See Arts. 56, 57, and 58.

RELATIONS BETWEEN THE TRIGONOMETRICAL FUNCTIONS OF THE SIDES AND THE ANGLES OF A SPHERICAL TRIANGLE

37. *To express the cosine of an angle of a triangle in terms of sines and cosines of the sides.*

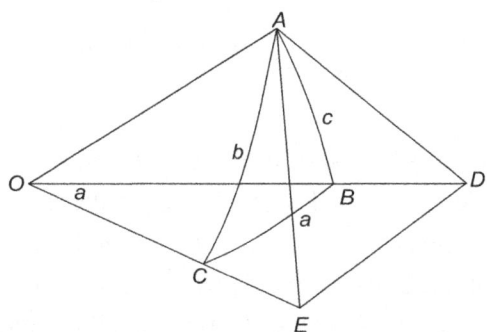

Let *ABC* be a spherical triangle, *O* the centre of the sphere. Let the tangent at *A* to the arc *AC* meet *OC* produced at *E*, and let the tangent at *A* to the arc *AB* meet *OB* produced at *D*; join *ED*. Thus the angle *EAD* is the angle *A* of the spherical triangle, and the angle *EOD* measures the side *a*.

From the triangles ADE and ODE we have

$$DE^2 = AD^2 + AE^2 - 2AD \cdot AE \cos A,$$

$$DE^2 = OD^2 + OE^2 - 2OD \cdot OE \cos a;$$

also the angles OAD and OAE are right angles, so that $OD^2 = OA^2 + AD^2$ and $OE^2 = OA^2 + AE^2$. Hence by subtraction we have

$$0 = 2OA^2 + 2AD \cdot AE \cos A - 2OD \cdot OE \cos a;$$

therefore

$$\cos a = \frac{OA}{OE} \cdot \frac{OA}{OD} + \frac{AE}{OE} \cdot \frac{AD}{OD} \cos A;$$

that is $\qquad \cos a = \cos b \cos c + \sin b \sin c \cos A.$

Therefore

$$\cos A = \frac{\cos a - \cos b \cos c}{\sin b \sin c}.$$

38. We have supposed, in the construction of the preceding Article, that the sides which contain the angle A are less than quadrants, for we have assumed that the tangents at A meet OB and OC respectively produced. We must now shew that the formulæ obtained is true when these sides are not less than quadrants. This we shall do by special examination of the cases in which one side or each side is greater than a quadrant or equal to a quadrant.

1. Suppose only one of the sides which contain the angle A to be greater than a quadrant, for example, AB. Produce BA and BC to meet at B'; and put $AB' = c'$, $CB' = a'$.

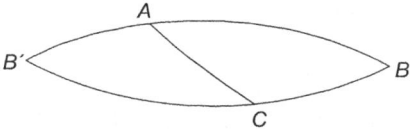

Then we have from the triangle $AB'C$, by what has been already proved,

$$\cos a' = \cos b \cos c' + \sin b \sin c' \cos B'AC;$$

but $a' = \pi - a, c' = \pi - c, B'AC = \pi - A$; thus

$$\cos a = \cos b \cos c + \sin b \sin c \cos A.$$

2. Suppose both the sides which contain the angle A to be greater than quadrants. Produce AB and AC to meet at A'; put $A'B = c'$, $A'C = b'$; then from the triangle $A'BC$, as before,

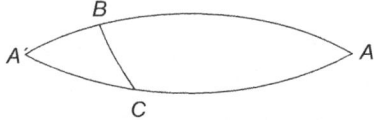

$$\cos a = \cos b' \cos c' + \sin b' \sin c' \cos A';$$

but $b' = \pi - b, c' = \pi - c, A' = A$; thus

$$\cos a = \cos b \cos c + \sin b \sin c \cos A.$$

3. Suppose that one of the sides which contain the angle A is a quadrant, for example, AB; on AC, produced if necessary, take AD equal to a quadrant and draw BD.

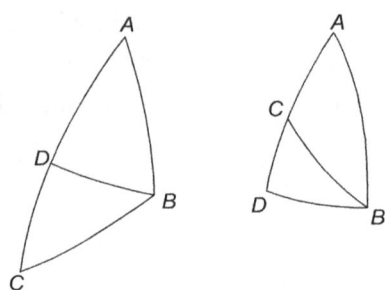

If *BD* is a quadrant *B* is a pole of *AC* (Art. 11); in this case $a = \dfrac{\pi}{2}$ and $A = \dfrac{\pi}{2}$ as well as $c = \dfrac{\pi}{2}$. Thus the formula to be verified reduces to the identity $0 = 0$. If *BD* be not a quadrant, the triangle *BDC* gives

$$\cos a = \cos CD \cos BD + \sin CD \sin BD \cos CDB,$$

and

$$\cos CDB = 0, \cos CD = \cos\left(\frac{\pi}{2} - b\right) = \sin b, \cos BD = \cos A;$$

thus $\qquad\qquad \cos a = \sin b \cos A;$

and this is what the formula in Art. 37 becomes when $c = \dfrac{\pi}{2}$.

4. Suppose that both the sides which contain the angle *A* are quadrants. The formula then becomes $\cos a = \cos A$; and this is obviously true, for *A* is now the pole of *BC*, and thus $A = a$.

Thus the formula in Art. 37 is proved to be universally true.

39. The formula in Art. 37 may be applied to express the cosine of any angle of a triangle in terms of sines and cosines of the sides; thus we have the three formulæ,

$$\cos a = \cos b \cos c + \sin b \sin c \cos A,$$

$$\cos b = \cos c \cos a + \sin c \sin a \cos B,$$

$$\cos c = \cos a \cos b + \sin a \sin b \cos C.$$

These may be considered as the fundamental equations of Spherical Trigonometry; we shall proceed to deduce various formulæ from them.

40. *To express the sine of an angle of a spherical triangle in terms of trigonometrical functions of the sides.*

We have

$$\cos A = \frac{\cos a - \cos b \cos c}{\sin b \sin c};$$

therefore

$$\sin^2 A = 1 - \left(\frac{\cos a - \cos b \cos c}{\sin b \sin c} \right)^2$$

$$= \frac{(1 - \cos^2 b)(1 - \cos^2 c) - (\cos a - \cos b \cos c)^2}{\sin^2 b \sin^2 c}$$

$$= \frac{1 - \cos^2 a - \cos^2 b - \cos^2 c + 2 \cos a \cos b \cos c}{\sin c^2 b \sin^2 c};$$

therefore

$$\sin A = \frac{\sqrt{(1 - \cos^2 a - \cos^2 b - \cos^2 c + 2\cos a \cos b \cos c)}}{\sin b \sin c}.$$

The radical on the right-hand side must be taken with the positive sign, because $\sin b$, $\sin c$, and $\sin A$ are all positive.

41.   From the value of $\sin A$ in the preceding Article it follows that

$$\frac{\sin A}{\sin a} = \frac{\sin B}{\sin b} = \frac{\sin C}{\sin c},$$

for each of these is equal to the same expression, namely,

$$\frac{\sqrt{1 - \cos^2 a - \cos^2 b - \cos^2 c + 2\cos a \cos b \cos c)}}{\sin a \sin b \sin c}.$$

Thus *the sines of the angles of a spherical triangle are proportional to the sines of the opposite sides*. We will give an independent proof of this proposition in the following Article.

42.   *The sines of the angles of a spherical triangle are proportional to the sines of the opposite sides.*

Let ABC be a spherical triangle, O the centre of the sphere. Take any point P in OA, draw PD perpendicular to the plane BOC, and from D draw DE,

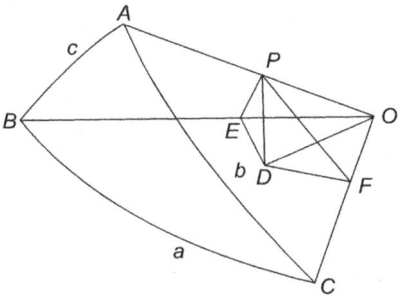

DF perpendicular to *OB*, *OC* respectively; join *PE*, *PF*, *OD*.

Since *PD* is perpendicular to the plane *BOC*, it makes right angles with every straight line meeting it in that plane; hence

$$PE^2 = PD^2 + DE^2 = PO^2 - OD^2 + DF^2 = PO^2 - OE^2;$$

thus *PEO* is a right angle. Therefore $PE = OP \sin POE = OP \sin c$; and $PD = PE \sin PED = PE \sin B = OP \sin c \sin B$.

Similarly, $PD = OP \sin b \sin C$; therefore

$$OP \sin c \sin B = OP \sin b \sin C;$$

therefore

$$\frac{\sin B}{\sin C} = \frac{\sin b}{\sin c}.$$

The figure supposes *b*, *c*, *B*, and *C* each less than a right angle; it will be found on examination that the proof will hold when the figure is modified to meet any case which can occur. If, for instance, *B* alone is greater than a right angle, the point *D* will fall beyond *OB* instead of between *OB* and *OC*; then *PED* will be the *supplement* of *B*, and thus sin *PED* is still equal to sin *B*.

43. *To shew that* $\cot a \sin b = \cot A \sin C + \cos b \cos C$.

We have

$$\cos a = \cos b \cos c + \sin b \sin c \cos A,$$
$$\cos c = \cos a \cos b + \sin a \sin \cos C,$$
$$\sin c = \sin a \frac{\sin C}{\sin A}.$$

Substitute the values of $\cos c$ and $\sin c$ in the first equation; thus

$$\cos a = (\cos a \cos b + \sin a \sin b \cos C) \cos b$$
$$+ \frac{\sin a \sin b \cos A \sin C}{\sin A};$$

by transposition

$$\cos a \sin^2 b = \sin a \sin b \cos b \cos C + \sin a \sin b \cot A \sin C;$$

divide by $\sin a \sin b$; thus

$$\cot a \sin b = \cos b \cos C + \cot A \sin C.$$

44. By interchanging the letters five other formulæ may be obtained like that in the preceding Article; the whole six formulæ will be as follows:

$$\cot a \sin b = \cot A \sin C + \cos b \cos C,$$
$$\cot b \sin a = \cot B \sin C + \cos a \cos C,$$
$$\cot b \sin c = \cot B \sin A + \cos c \cos A,$$
$$\cot c \sin b = \cot C \sin A + \cos b \cos A,$$

$$\cot c \sin a = \cot C \sin B + \cos a \cos B,$$

$$\cot a \sin c = \cot A \sin B + \cos c \cos B.$$

45. *To express the sine, cosine, and tangent, of half an angle of a triangle as functions of the sides.*

We have, by Art. 37, $\cos A = \dfrac{\cos a - \cos b \cos c}{\sin b \sin c};$

therefore

$$1 - \cos A = 1 - \frac{\cos a - \cos b \cos c}{\sin b \sin c} = \frac{\cos(b-c) - \cos a}{\sin b \sin c};$$

therefore

$$\sin^2 \frac{A}{2} = \frac{\sin \frac{1}{2}(a+b-c) \sin \frac{1}{2}(a-b+c)}{\sin b \sin c}.$$

Let $2s = a + b + c$, so that s is half the sum of the sides of the triangle; then

$$a + b - c = 2s - 2c = 2(s - c), \quad a - b + c = 2s - 2b = 2(s - b);$$

thus, $\sin^2 \dfrac{A}{2} = \dfrac{\sin(s-b)\sin(s-c)}{\sin b \sin c},$

and $\sin \dfrac{A}{2} = \sqrt{\left\{ \dfrac{\sin(s-b)\sin(s-c)}{\sin b \sin c} \right\}}$

Also,

$$1 + \cos A = 1 + \frac{\cos a - \cos b \cos c}{\sin b \sin c} = \frac{\cos a - \cos(b+c)}{\sin b \sin c};$$

therefore

$$\cos^2 \frac{A}{2} = \frac{\sin \frac{1}{2}(a+b+c)\sin \frac{1}{2}(b+c-a)}{\sin b \sin c} = \frac{\sin s \sin(s-a)}{\sin b \sin c},$$

and

$$\cos \frac{A}{2} = \sqrt{\left\{ \frac{\sin s \sin(s-a)}{\sin b \sin c} \right\}}$$

From the expressions for $\sin \dfrac{A}{2}$ and $\cos \dfrac{A}{2}$ we deduce

$$\tan \frac{A}{2} = \sqrt{\left\{ \frac{\sin(s-b)\sin(s-c)}{\sin s \sin(s-a)} \right\}}.$$

The positive sign must be given to the radicals which occur in this Article, because $\dfrac{A}{2}$ is less than a right angle, and therefore its sine, cosine, and tangent are all positive.

46.   Since $\sin A = 2\sin \dfrac{A}{2}\cos \dfrac{A}{2}$, we obtain

$$\sin A = \frac{2}{\sin b \sin c}\{\sin s \sin(s-a)\sin(s-b)\sin(s-c)\}^{\frac{1}{2}}.$$

It may be shewn that the expression for $\sin A$ in Art. 40 agrees with the present expression by putting the numerator of that expression in factors, as in *Plane Trigonometry*, Art. 115.

We shall find it convenient to use a symbol for the radical in the value of sin A; we shall denote it by n, so that

$$n^2 = \sin s \sin(s-a) \sin(s-b) \sin(s-c),$$

and $4n^2 = 1 - \cos^2 a - \cos^2 b - \cos^2 c + 2\cos a \cos b \cos c.$

47. *To express the cosine of a side of a triangle in terms of sines and cosines of the angles.*

In the formula of Art. 37 we may, by Art. 28, change the sides into the supplements of the corresponding angles and the angle into the supplement of the corresponding side; thus

$$\cos(\pi - A) = \cos(\pi - B)\cos(\pi - C) + \sin(\pi - B)$$
$$\sin(\pi - C)\cos(\pi - a),$$

that is, $\cos A = -\cos B \cos C + \sin B \sin C \cos a.$

Similarly $\cos B = -\cos C \cos A + \sin C \sin A \cos b,$

and $\cos C = -\cos A \cos B + \sin A \sin B \cos c.$

48. The formulæ in Art. 44 will of course remain true when the angles and sides are changed into the supplements of the corresponding sides and angles respectively; it will be found, however, that no *new* formulæ are thus obtained, but only the *same* formulæ over again. This consideration will furnish some assistance in retaining those formulæ accurately in the memory.

49. *To express the sine, cosine, and tangent, of half a side of a triangle as functions of the angles.*

We have, by Art. 47,

$$\cos a = \frac{\cos A + \cos B \cos C}{\sin B \sin C};$$

therefore

$$1 - \cos a = 1 - \frac{\cos A + \cos B \cos C}{\sin B \sin C} = \frac{\cos A + \cos(B+C)}{\sin B \sin C};$$

therefore $\sin^2 \dfrac{a}{2} = -\dfrac{\cos \frac{1}{2}(A+B+C)\cos \frac{1}{2}(B+C-A)}{\sin B \sin C}.$

Let $2S = A + B + C$; then $B + C - A = 2(S - A)$, therefore

$$\sin^2 \frac{a}{2} = -\frac{\cos S \cos(S-A)}{\sin B \sin C},$$

and $\qquad \sin \dfrac{a}{2} = \sqrt{\left\{ -\dfrac{\cos S \cos(S-A)}{\sin B \sin C} \right\}}.$

Also

$$1 + \cos a = 1 + \frac{\cos A + \cos B \cos C}{\sin B \sin C} = \frac{\cos A + \cos(B-C)}{\sin B \sin C};$$

therefore

$$\cos^2 \frac{a}{2} = \frac{\cos \frac{1}{2}(A-B+C)\cos \frac{1}{2}(A+B-C)}{\sin B \sin C}$$
$$= \frac{\cos(S-B)\cos(S-C)}{\sin B \sin C},$$

and
$$\cos\frac{a}{2} = \sqrt{\left\{\frac{\cos(S-B)\cos(S-C)}{\sin B \sin C}\right\}}.$$

Hence

$$\tan\frac{a}{2} = \sqrt{\left\{-\frac{\cos S \cos(S-A)}{\cos(S-B)\cos(S-C)}\right\}}.$$

The positive sign must be given to the radicals which occur in this Article, because $\dfrac{a}{2}$ is less than a right angle.

50.   The expressions in the preceding Article may also be obtained immediately from those given in Art. 45 by means of Art. 28.

It may be remarked that the values of $\sin\dfrac{a}{2}, \cos\dfrac{a}{2}$, and $\tan\dfrac{a}{2}$ are *real*. For S is greater than one right angle and less than three right angles by Art. 32; therefore $\cos S$ is *negative*. And in the polar triangle any side is less than the sum of the other two; thus $\pi - A$ is less than $\pi - B + \pi - C$; therefore $B + C - A$ is less than π; therefore $S - A$ is less than $\dfrac{\pi}{2}$, and $B + C - A$ is algebraically greater than $-\pi$, so that $S - A$ is algebraically greater than $-\dfrac{\pi}{2}$; therefore $\cos(S-A)$ *is positive*. Similarly also $\cos(S-B)$ and $\cos(S-C)$ are positive. Hence the values of $\sin\dfrac{a}{2}, \cos\dfrac{a}{2}$, and $\tan\dfrac{a}{2}$ are real.

51.   Since $\sin a = 2\sin\dfrac{a}{2}\cos\dfrac{a}{2}$, we obtain

$$\sin a = \frac{2}{\sin B \sin C} \{-\cos S \cos(S-A)\cos(S-B)\cos(s-c)\}^{\frac{1}{2}}.$$

We shall use N for

$$\{-\cos S \cos(S-A)\cos(S-B)\cos(S-C)\}^{\frac{1}{2}}.$$

52. *To demonstrate Napier's Analogies.*

We have

$$\frac{\sin A}{\sin a} = \frac{\sin B}{\sin b} = m \text{ suppose;}$$

then, by a theorem of Algebra,

$$m = \frac{\sin A + \sin B}{\sin a + \sin b}, \qquad (1)$$

and also $\qquad m = \dfrac{\sin A - \sin B}{\sin a - \sin b}. \qquad (2)$

Now

$$\cos A + \cos B \cos C = \sin B \sin C \cos a = m \sin C \sin b \cos a,$$

and

$$\cos B + \cos A \cos C = \sin A \sin C \cos b = m \sin C \sin a \cos b,$$

therefore, by addition,

$$(\cos A + \cos B)(1 + \cos C) = m \sin C \sin(a + b); \qquad (3)$$

therefore by (1) we have

$$\frac{\sin A + \sin B}{\cos A \cos B} = \frac{\sin a + \sin b}{\sin(a+b)} \frac{1 + \cos C}{\sin C},$$

that is,

$$\tan\frac{1}{2}(A+B) = \frac{\cos\frac{1}{2}(a-b)}{\cos\frac{1}{2}(a+b)}\cot\frac{C}{2}. \tag{4}$$

Similarly from (3) and (2) we have

$$\frac{\sin A - \sin B}{\cos A + \cos B} = \frac{\sin a - \sin b}{\sin(a+b)} \frac{1 + \cos C}{\sin C},$$

that is,

$$\tan\frac{1}{2}(A-B) = \frac{\sin\frac{1}{2}(a-b)}{\sin\frac{1}{2}(a+b)}\cot\frac{C}{2}. \tag{5}$$

By writing $\pi - A$ for a, and so on in (4) and (5) we obtain

$$\tan\frac{1}{2}(a+b) = \frac{\cos\frac{1}{2}(A-B)}{\cos\frac{1}{2}(A+B)}\tan\frac{c}{2}, \tag{6}$$

$$\tan\frac{1}{2}(a-b) = \frac{\sin\frac{1}{2}(A-B)}{\sin\frac{1}{2}(A+B)}\tan\frac{c}{2}. \tag{7}$$

The formulæ (4), (5), (6), (7) may be put in the form of proportions or analogies, and are called from their discoverer *Napier's Analogies*: the last two may be demonstrated without recurring to the polar triangle by starting with the formulæ in Art. 39.

53. In equation (4) of the preceding Article, $\cos\frac{1}{2}(a-b)$ and $\cot\dfrac{C}{2}$ are necessarily positive quantities; hence the equation shews that $\tan\dfrac{1}{2}(A+B)$ and $\cos\dfrac{1}{2}(a+b)$ are of the same sign; thus $\dfrac{1}{2}(A+B)$ and $\dfrac{1}{2}(a+b)$ are either both less than a right angle or both greater than a right angle. This is expressed by saying that $\dfrac{1}{2}(A+B)$ and $\dfrac{1}{2}(a+b)$ *are of the same affection*.

54. *To demonstrate Delambre's Analogies*.

We have $\cos c = \cos a \cos b + \sin a \sin b \cos C$; therefore

$$1+\cos c = 1 + \cos a \cos b + \sin a \sin b \left(\cos^2\frac{1}{2}C - \sin^2\frac{1}{2}C \right)$$

$$= \{1+\cos(a-b)\}\cos^2\frac{1}{2}C + \{1+\cos(a+b)\}\sin^2\frac{1}{2}C;$$

therefore

$$\cos^2\frac{1}{2}c = \cos^2\frac{1}{2}(a-b)\cos^2\frac{1}{2}C + \cos^2\frac{1}{2}(a+b)\sin^2\frac{1}{2}C.$$

$$\sin^2\frac{1}{2}c = \sin^2\frac{1}{2}(a-b)\cos^2\frac{1}{2}C + \sin^2\frac{1}{2}(a+b)\sin^2\frac{1}{2}C.$$

Now add unity to the square of each member of Napier's first two analogies; hence by the formulæ just proved

$$\sec^2 \frac{1}{2}(A+B) = \frac{\cos^2 \frac{1}{2}c}{\cos^2 \frac{1}{2}(a+b)\sin^2 \frac{1}{2}C},$$

$$\sec^2 \frac{1}{2}(A-B) = \frac{\sin^2 \frac{1}{2}C}{\sin^2 \frac{1}{2}(a+b)\sin^2 \frac{1}{2}C}.$$

Extract the square roots; thus, since $\frac{1}{2}(A+B)$ and $\frac{1}{2}(a+b)$ are of the same affection, we obtain

$$\cos\frac{1}{2}(A+B)\cos\frac{1}{2}c = \cos\frac{1}{2}(a+b)\sin\frac{1}{2}C, \qquad (1)$$

$$\cos\frac{1}{2}(A-B)\sin\frac{1}{2}c = \sin\frac{1}{2}(a+b)\sin\frac{1}{2}C. \qquad (2)$$

Multiply the first two of Napier's analogies respectively by these results; thus

$$\sin\frac{1}{2}(A+B)\cos\frac{1}{2}c = \cos\frac{1}{2}(a-b)\cos\frac{1}{2}C, \qquad (3)$$

$$\sin\frac{1}{2}(A-B)\sin\frac{1}{2}c = \sin\frac{1}{2}(a-b)\cos\frac{1}{2}C. \qquad (4)$$

The last four formulæ are commonly, but improperly, called *Gauss's Theorems*; they were first given by Delambre in the *Connaissance des Tems* for 1809, page 445. See the *Philosophical Magazine* for February, 1873.

55. The properties of supplemental triangles were proved geometrically in Art. 27, and by means of these properties the formulæ in Art. 47 were obtained; but these formulæ may be deduced analytically from those in Art. 39, and thus the

whole subject may be made to depend on the formulæ of Art. 39.

For from Art. 39 we obtain expressions for cos A, cos B, cos C; and from these we find

$$\cos A + \cos B \cos C = \frac{(\cos a - \cos b \cos c)\sin^2 a + (\cos b - \cos a \cos c)(\cos c - \cos a \cos b)}{\sin^2 a \sin b \sin c}.$$

In the numerator of this fraction write $1 - \cos^2 a$ for $\sin^2 a$; thus the numerator will be found to reduce to

$\cos a(1 - \cos^2 a - \cos^2 b - \cos^2 c + 2 \cos a \cos b \cos c)$,

and this is equal to $\cos a \sin B \sin C \sin^2 a \sin b \sin c$, (Art. 41); therefore

$\cos A + \cos B \cos C - \cos a \sin B \sin C.$

Similarly the other two corresponding formulæ may be proved.

Thus the formulæ in Art. 47 are established; and therefore, without assuming the existence and properties of the Polar Triangle, we deduce the following theorem: *If the sides and angles of a spherical triangle be changed respectively into the supplements of the corresponding angles and sides, the fundamental formulæ of Art. 39 hold good, and therefore also all results deducible from them.*

56. The formulæ in the present Chapter may be applied to establish analytically various propositions respecting spherical triangles which either have been proved geometrically in the preceding

Chapter, or may be so proved. Thus, for example, the second of Napier's analogies is

$$\tan\frac{1}{2}(A-B) = \frac{\sin\frac{1}{2}(a-b)}{\sin\frac{1}{2}(a+b)}\cot\frac{C}{2};$$

this shews that $\frac{1}{2}(A-B)$ is positive, negative, or zero, according as $\frac{1}{2}(a-b)$ is positive, negative, or zero; thus we obtain all the results included in Arts. 33. . . 36.

57. *If two triangles have two sides of the one equal to two sides of the other, each to each, and likewise the included angles equal, then their other angles will be equal, each to each, and likewise their bases will be equal.*

We may shew that the bases are equal by applying the first formula in Art. 39 to each triangle, supposing b, c, and A the same in the two triangles; then the remaining two formulæ of Art. 39 will shew that B and C are the same in the two triangles.

It should be observed that the two triangles in this case are not necessarily such that one may be made to coincide with *the other by superposition*. The sides of one may be equal to those of the other, each to each, but in a reverse order, as in the following figures.

Two triangles which are equal in this manner are said to be *symmetrically* equal; when they are equal so as to admit of superposition they are said to be *absolutely* equal.

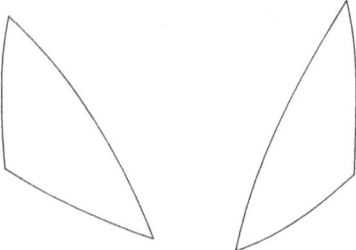

58. *If two spherical triangles have two sides of the one equal to two sides of the other, each to each, but the angle which is contained by the two sides of the one greater than the angle which is contained by the two sides which are equal to them of the other, the base of that which has the greater angle will be greater than the base of the other; and conversely.*

Let b and c denote the sides which are equal in the two triangles; let a be the base and A the opposite angle of one triangle, and a' and A' similar quantities for the other. Then

$$\cos a = \cos b \cos c + \sin b \sin c \cos A,$$

$$\cos a' = \cos b \cos c + \sin b \sin c \cos A';$$

therefore $\cos a - \cos a' + \sin b \sin c(\cos A - \cos A')$;

that is,

$$\sin \frac{1}{2}(a+a')\sin \frac{1}{2}(a-a') = \sin b \sin c \sin \frac{1}{2}(A+A')$$
$$\sin \frac{1}{2}(A-A');$$

this shews that $\frac{1}{2}(a-a')$ and $\frac{1}{2}(A-A')$ are of the same sign.

59. *If on a sphere any point be taken within a circle which is not its pole, of all the arcs which can be drawn from that point to the circumference, the greatest is that in which the pole is, and the other part of that produced is the least; and of any others, that which is nearer to the greatest is always greater than one more remote; and from the same point to the circumference there can be drawn only two arcs which are equal to each other, and these make equal angles with the shortest arc on opposite sides of it.*

This follows readily from the preceding three Articles.

60. We will give another proof of the fundamental formulæ in Art. 39, which is very simple, requiring only a knowledge of the elements of Co-ordinate Geometry.

Suppose ABC any spherical triangle, O the centre of the sphere, take O as the origin of co-ordinates, and let the axis of z pass through C. Let x_1, y_1, z_1 be the co-ordinates of A, and x^2, y^2, z^2 those of B; let r be the radius of the sphere. Then the square on the straight line AB is equal to

$$(x_1 - x_2)^2 + (y_1 - y_2)^2 + (z_1 - z_2)^2,$$

and also to $r^2 + r^2 - 2r^2 \cos AOB$;

and $x_1^2 + y_1^2 + z_1^2 = r^2, x_2^2 + y_2^2 + z_2^2 = r^2$, thus

$$x_1 x_2 + y_1 y_2 + z_1 z_2 = r^2 \cos AOB.$$

Now make the usual substitutions in passing from rectangular to polar co-ordinates, namely,

$$z_1 = r\cos\theta_1, \quad x_1 = r\sin\theta_1, \cos\phi_1, \quad y_1 = r\sin\theta_1, \sin\phi_1,$$
$$z_2 = r\cos\theta_2, \quad x_2 = r\sin\theta_2, \cos\phi_2, \quad y_2 = r\sin\theta_2, \sin\phi_2;$$

thus we obtain

$$\cos\theta_2\cos\theta_1 + \sin\theta_2\sin\theta_1\cos(\phi_1 - \phi_2) = \cos AOB,$$

that is, in the ordinary notation of Spherical Trigonometry,

$$\cos a\cos b + \sin a\sin b\cos C = \cos c.$$

This method has the advantage of giving a *perfectly general proof*, as all the equations used are universally true.

EXAMPLES

1. If $A = a$, shew that B and b are equal or supplemental, as also C and c.

2. If one angle of a triangle be equal to the sum of the other two, the greatest side is double of the distance of its middle point from the opposite angle.

3. When does the polar triangle coincide with the primitive triangle?

4. If D be the middle point of AB, shew that

$$\cos AC + \cos BC = 2\cos\frac{1}{2}AB\cos CD.$$

5. If two angles of a spherical triangle be respectively equal to the sides opposite to them, shew that the remaining side is the supplement of the remaining angle; or else that the triangle has two quadrants and two right angles, and then the remaining side is equal to the remaining angle.

6. In an equilateral triangle, shew that $2\cos\dfrac{a}{2}\sin\dfrac{A}{2}=1$.

7. In an equilateral triangle, shew that $\tan^2\dfrac{a}{2}=1-2\cos A$; hence deduce the limits between which the sides and the angles of an equilateral triangle are restricted.

8. In an equilateral triangle, shew that $\sec A = 1 + \sec a$.

9. If the three sides of a spherical triangle be halved and a new triangle formed, the angle θ between the new sides $\dfrac{b}{2}$ and $\dfrac{c}{2}$ is given by $\cos\theta = \cos A + \dfrac{1}{2}\tan\dfrac{b}{2}\tan\dfrac{c}{2}\sin^2\theta$.

10. AB, CD are quadrants on the surface of a sphere intersecting at E, the extremities being joined by great circles: shew that

$$\cos AEC = \cos AC \cos BD - \cos BC \cos AD.$$

11. If $b = c = \pi$, shew that $\sin 2B + \sin 2C = 0$.

12. If DE be an arc of a great circle bisecting the sides AB, AC of a spherical triangle at D and E, P a pole of DE, and PB, PD, PE, PC be joined by arcs of great circles, shew that the angle BPC = twice the angle DPE.

13. In a spherical triangle shew that

$$\sin b \sin c = \cos b \cos c \cos A$$
$$= \sin B \sin C - \cos B \cos C \cos a.$$

14. If D be any point in the side BC of a triangle, shew that

$$\cos AD \sin BC = \cos AB \sin DC + \cos AC \sin BD.$$

15. In a spherical triangle shew that θ, ϕ, ψ be the lengths of arcs of great circles drawn from A, B, C perpendicular to the opposite sides,

$$\sin a \sin \theta = \sin b \sin \phi = \sin c \sin \psi$$

$$= \sqrt{(1 - \cos^2 a - \cos^2 b - \cos^2 c + 2 \cos a \cos b \cos c)}.$$

16. In a spherical triangle, if, θ, ϕ, ψ be the arcs bisecting the angles A, B, C respectively and terminated by the opposite sides, shew that

$$\cot \theta \cos \frac{A}{2} + \cot \phi \cos \frac{B}{2} + \cot \psi \cos \frac{C}{2} = \cot a + \cot b + \cot c.$$

17. Two ports are in the same parallel of latitude, their common latitude being λ and their difference of longitude 2λ shew that the saving of distance in sailing from one to the other on the great circle, instead of sailing due East or West, is

$$2r\{\lambda - \cos l - \sin^{-1}(\sin \lambda \cos l)\},$$

λ being expressed in circular measure, and r being the radius of the Earth.

18. If a ship be proceeding uniformly along a great circle and the observed latitudes be l_1, l_2, l_3, at equal intervals of time, in each of which the distance traversed is s, shew that

$$s = r \cos^{-1} \frac{\sin \frac{1}{2}(l_1 + l_3)\cos \frac{1}{2}(l_1 - l_3)}{\sin l_2},$$

r denoting the Earth's radius: and shew that the change of longitude may also be found in terms of the three latitudes.

SOLUTION OF RIGHT-ANGLED TRIANGLES

61. In every spherical triangle there are six elements, namely, the three sides and the three angles, besides the radius of the sphere, which is supposed constant. The solution of spherical triangles is the process by which, when the values of a sufficient number of the six elements are given, we calculate the values of the remaining elements. It will appear, as we proceed, that when the values of three of the elements are given, those of the remaining three can generally be found. We begin with the right-angled triangle: here two elements, in addition to the right angle, will be supposed known.

62. The formulæ requisite for the solution of right-angled triangles may be obtained from the preceding Chapter by supposing one of the angles a right angle, as C for example. They may also be obtained very easily in an independent manner, as we will now shew.

Let *ABC* be a spherical triangle having a right angle at *C*; let *O* be the centre of the sphere. From any point *P* in *OA* draw *PM* perpendicular to *OC*, and from *M* draw *MN* perpendicular to *OB*, and join *PN*. Then *PM* is perpendicular to *MN*, because the plane *AOC* is perpendicular to the plane *BOC*; hence

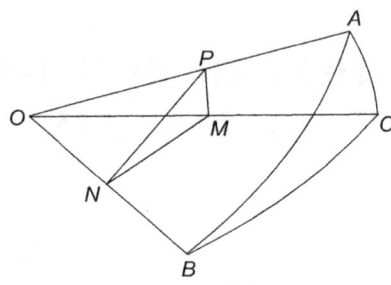

$$PN^2 = PM^2 + MN^2 = OP^2 - OM^2 + OM^2 - ON^2 = OP^2 - ON^2;$$

therefore *PNO* is a right angle. And

$$\frac{ON}{OP} = \frac{ON}{OM} \cdot \frac{OM}{OP}, \text{that is, } \cos c = \cos a \cos b, \qquad (1)$$

$$\left.\begin{aligned} \frac{PM}{OP} &= \frac{PM}{PN} \cdot \frac{PN}{OP}, \text{that is, } \sin b = \sin B \sin c \\ \text{Similarly, } \sin a &= \sin A \sin c \end{aligned}\right\}, \qquad (2)$$

$$\left.\begin{aligned} \frac{MN}{ON} &= \frac{MN}{PN} \cdot \frac{PN}{ON}, \text{that is, } \tan a = \cos B \tan c \\ \text{Similarly, } \tan b &= \cos A \tan c \end{aligned}\right\}, \qquad (3)$$

$$\left.\begin{aligned} \frac{PM}{OM} &= \frac{PM}{MN} \cdot \frac{MN}{OM}, \text{that is, } \tan b = \tan B \sin a \\ \text{Similarly, } \tan a &= \tan A \sin b \end{aligned}\right\}. \qquad (4)$$

Multiply together the two formulæ (4); thus,

$$\tan A \, \tan B = \frac{\tan a \tan b}{\sin a \sin b} = \frac{1}{\cos a \cos b} = \frac{1}{\cos c} \text{ by } (1);$$

therefore $\qquad \cos c = \cot A \cot B.$ $\qquad\qquad$ (5)

Multiply crosswise the second formula in (2) and the first in (3); thus $\sin a \cos B \tan c = \tan a \sin A \sin c$;

therefore $\qquad \cos B = \dfrac{\sin A \cos c}{\cos a} = \sin A \cos b \text{ by } (1).$

Thus $\qquad\qquad\qquad\qquad\qquad \cos B = \sin A \cos b$
Similarly $\qquad\qquad\qquad\qquad \cos A = \sin B \cos a$ $\qquad$ (6)

These six formulæ comprise ten equations; and thus we can solve every case of right-angled triangles. For every one of these ten equations is a distinct combination involving three out of the five quantities a, b, c, A, B; and out of five quantities only ten combinations of three can be formed. Thus any two of the five quantities being given and a third required, some one of the preceding ten equations will serve to determine that third quantity.

63. As we have stated, the above six formulæ may be obtained from those given in the preceding Chapter by supposing C a right angle. Thus (1) follows from Art. 39, (2) from Art. 41, (3) from the fourth and fifth equations of Art. 44, (4) from the first and second equations of Art. 44, (5) from the third equation of Art. 47, (6) from the first and second equations of Art. 47.

Since the six formulæ may be obtained from those given in the preceding Chapter which have been proved to be universally true, we do not stop to shew that the demonstration of Art. 62 may be applied to every case which can occur; the student may for exercise investigate the modifications which will be necessary when we suppose one or more of the quantities *a, b, c, A, B* equal to a right angle or greater than a right angle.

64. Certain properties of right-angled triangles are deducible from the formulæ of Art. 62.

From (1) it follows that cos *c* has the same sign as the product cos *a* cos *b*; hence either all the cosines are positive, or else only one is positive. Therefore *in a right-angled triangle either all the three sides are less than quadrants, or else one side is less than a quadrant and the other two sides are greater than quadrants.*

From (4) it follows that tan *a* has the same sign as tan *A*. Therefore *A* and *a* are either both greater than $\frac{\pi}{2}$, or both less than $\frac{\pi}{2}$; this is expressed by saying that *A* and *a* are of the *same affection*. Similarly *B* and *b* are of the same affection.

65. The formulæ of Art. 62 are comprised in the following enunciations, which the student will find it useful to remember; the results are distinguished by the same numbers as have

been already applied to them in Art. 62; the side opposite the right angle is called the *hypotenuse*:

cos hyp   = product of cosines of sides   (1),

cos hyp   = product of cotangents of angles   (5),

sine side = sine of opposite angle × sine hyp   (2),

tan side = tan hyp × cos included angle   (3),

tan side = tan opposite angle × sine of other side (4),

cos angle = cos opposite side × sine of other angle (6).

66. *Napier's Rules*. The formulæ of Art. 62 are comprised in two rules, which are called, from their inventor, *Napier's Rules of Circular Parts*. Napier was also the inventor of Logarithms, and the Rules of Circular Parts were first published by him in a work entitled *Mirifici Logarithmorum Canonis Descriptio* ... Edinburgh, 1614. These rules we will now explain.

The right angle is left out of consideration; the two sides which include the right angle, the complement of the hypotenuse, and the complements of the other angles are called the *circular parts* of the triangle. Thus there are *five* circular parts, namely,

$a, b, \dfrac{\pi}{2} - A, \dfrac{\pi}{2} - c, \dfrac{\pi}{2} - B$; and these are supposed to be ranged round a circle in the order in which they naturally occur with respect to the triangle.

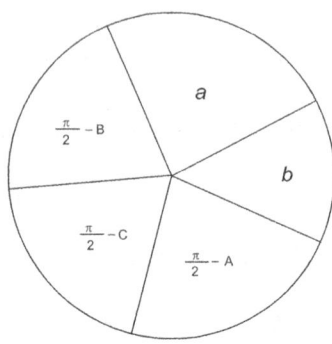

Any one of the five parts may be selected and called the *middle part*, then the two parts next to it are called *adjacent parts*, and the remaining two parts are called *opposite parts*.

For example, if $\dfrac{\pi}{2} - B$ is selected as the middle part, then the adjacent parts are a and $\dfrac{\pi}{2} - c$, and the opposite parts are b and $\dfrac{\pi}{2} - A$.

Then Napier's Rules are the following:

sine of the middle part = product of tangents of adjacent parts,

sine of the middle part = product of cosines of opposite parts.

67. Napier's Rules may be demonstrated by shewing that they agree with the results already established. The following table shews the required agreement: in the first column are given the *middle parts*, in the second column the results of Napier's Rules, and in the third column the same results expressed as in Art. 62, with the number for reference used in that Article.

$$\frac{\pi}{2} - c \sin\left(\frac{\pi}{2} - c\right) = \tan\left(\frac{\pi}{2} - A\right) \tan\left(\frac{\pi}{2} - B\right)$$

$$\cos c = \cot A \cot B \quad (5),$$

$$\sin\left(\frac{\pi}{2} - c\right) = \cos a \cos b \qquad \cos c = \cos a \cos b \quad (1),$$

$$\frac{\pi}{2} - B \sin\left(\frac{\pi}{2} - B\right) = \tan a \tan\left(\frac{\pi}{2} - c\right)$$

$$\cos B = \tan a \cot c \quad (3),$$

$$\sin\left(\frac{\pi}{2} - B\right) = \cos b \cos\left(\frac{\pi}{2} - A\right) \qquad \cos B = \cos b \sin A \quad (6)$$

$$a \quad \sin a = \tan b \tan\left(\frac{\pi}{2} - B\right) \qquad \sin a = \tan b \cot B \quad (4)$$

$$\sin a = \cos\left(\frac{\pi}{2} - A\right) \cos\left(\frac{\pi}{2} - c\right) \quad \sin a = \sin A \sin c \quad (2),$$

$$b \quad \sin b = \tan\left(\frac{\pi}{2} - A\right) \tan a \qquad \sin b = \cot A \tan a \quad (4),$$

$$\sin b = \cos\left(\frac{\pi}{2} - B\right) \cos\left(\frac{\pi}{2} - c\right) \quad \sin b = \sin B \sin c \quad (2),$$

$$\frac{\pi}{2} - A \sin\left(\frac{\pi}{2} - A\right) = \tan b \tan\left(\frac{\pi}{2} - c\right)$$

$$\cos A = \tan b \cot c \quad (3),$$

$$\sin\left(\frac{\pi}{2} - A\right) = \cos a \cos\left(\frac{\pi}{2} - B\right) \qquad \cos A = \cos a \sin B \quad (6)$$

The last four cases need not have been given, since it is obvious that they are only repetitions of what had previously been given; the seventh and eighth are repetitions of the fifth and sixth, and the ninth and tenth are repetitions of the third and fourth.

68. It has been sometimes stated that the method of the preceding Article is the only one by which Napier's Rules can be demonstrated; this statement, however, is inaccurate, since besides this method Napier himself indicated another method of proof in his *Mirifici Logarithmorum Canonis Descriptio*, pp. 32, 35. This we will now briefly explain.

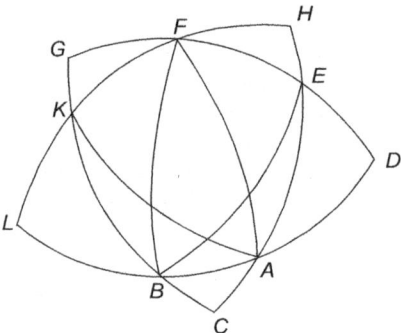

Let *ABC* be a spherical triangle right-angled at *C*; with *B* as pole describe a great circle *DEFG*, and with *A* as pole describe a great circle *HFKL*, and produce the sides of the original triangle *ABC* to meet these great circles. Then since *B* is a pole of *DEFG* the angles at *D* and *G* are right angles, and since *A* is a pole of *HFKL* the angles at *H* and *L* are right angles. Hence the five triangles *BAC, AED, EFH, FKG, KBL* are all *right-angled*; and moreover it will be found on examination that, although the elements of these triangles are different, *yet their circular parts are the same.* We will consider, for example, the triangle *AED*; the angle *EAD* is equal to the angle *BAC*, the side *AD* is the complement of *AB*; as the angles at *C* and *G* are right angles *E* is a pole of *GC* (Art. 13), therefore *EA* is the complement of *AC*; as *B* is a pole of *DE* the angle *BED* is a right angle, therefore the angle *AED* is the complement of the angle *BEC*, that is, the angle *AED* is the complement of the side *BC* (Art. 12); and similarly the side *DE* is equal to the angle *DBE*, and is therefore the complement of the angle *ABC*. Hence, if we denote the elements of the triangle *ABC* as usual by a, b, c, A, B, we have in the triangle *AED* the hypotenuse equal to $\frac{\pi}{2} - b$, the angles equal to A and $\frac{\pi}{2} - a$, and the sides respectively opposite these angles equal to $\frac{\pi}{2} - B$ and $\frac{\pi}{2} - c$. The *circular parts of AED* are therefore the same as those of *ABC*. Similarly the remaining three of the five right-angled triangles may be shewn to have the same circular parts as the triangle *ABC* has.

Now take *two* of the theorems in Art. 65, for example (1) and (3); then the truth of the *ten* cases comprised in Napier's Rules will be found to follow from applying the two theorems in succession to the five triangles formed in the preceding figure. Thus this method of considering Napier's Rules regards each Rule, not as the statement of dissimilar properties of one triangle, but as the statement of similar properties of five allied triangles.

69. In Napier's work a figure is given of which that in the preceding Article is a copy, except that different letters are used; Napier

briefly intimates that the truth of the Rules can be easily seen by means of this figure, as well as by the method of induction from consideration of all the cases which can occur. The late T. S. Davies, in his edition of Dr Hutton's *Course of Mathematics*, drew attention to Napier's own views and expanded the demonstration by a systematic examination of the figure of the preceding Article.

It is however easy to evade the necessity of examining the whole figure; all that is wanted is to observe the connexion between the triangle AED and the triangle BAC. For let a_1, a_2, a_3, a_4, a_5 represent the elements of the triangle BAC taken in order, beginning with the hypotenuse and omitting the right angle; then the elements of the triangle AED taken in order, beginning with the hypotenuse and omitting the right angle, are $\dfrac{\pi}{2} - a_3$, $\dfrac{\pi}{2} - a_4$, $\dfrac{\pi}{2} - a_5$, $\dfrac{\pi}{2} - a_1$, and a_2. If, therefore, to characterise the former we introduce a new set of quantities p_1, p_2, p_3, p_4, p_5, such that $a_1 + p_1 = a_2 + p_2 = a_5 + p_5 = \dfrac{\pi}{2}$, and that $p_3 = a_3$ and $p_4 = a_4$, then the original triangle being characterised by p_1, p_2, p_3, p_4, p_5, the second triangle will be similarly characterised by p_3, p_4, p_5, p_1, p_2. As the second triangle can give rise to a third in like manner, and so on, we see that every right-angled triangle is one of a system of five such triangles which are all characterised by the quantities p_1, p_2, p_3, p_4, p_5, always taken in order, each quantity in its turn standing first.

The late R.L. Ellis pointed out this connexion between the five triangles, and thus gave the true significance of Napier's Rules.

The memoir containing Mr Ellis's investigations, which was unpublished when the first edition of the present work appeared, will be found in pages 328...335 of *The Mathematical and other writings of Robert Leslie Ellis...* Cambridge, 1863.

Napier's own method of considering his Rules was neglected by writers on the subject until the late T. S. Davies drew attention to it. Hence, as we have already remarked in Art. 68, an erroneous statement was made respecting the Rules. For instance, Woodhouse says, in his *Trigonometry*: "There is no separate and independent proof of these rules;. ..." Airy says, in the treatise on Trigonometry in the *Encyclopædia Metropolitana*: "These rules are proved to be true only by showing that they comprehend all the equations which we have just found."

70. Opinions have differed with respect to the *utility* of Napier's Rules in practice. Thus Woodhouse says, "In the whole compass of mathematical science there cannot be found, perhaps, rules which more completely attain that which is the proper object of rules, namely, facility and brevity of computation." (*Trigonometry*, chapter 10) On the other hand may be set the following sentence from Airy's Trigonometry (*Encyclopædia Metropolitana*): "In the opinion of Delambre (and no one was better qualified by experience to give an opinion) these theorems are best recollected by the practical calculator in their unconnected form." See Delambre's *Astronomie*, vol. I. p. 205. Professor De Morgan strongly objects to Napier's Rules, and says (*Spherical Trigonometry*, Art. 17): "There are certain mnemonical

formulæ called *Napier's Rules of Circular Parts*, which are generally explained. We do not give them, because we are convinced that they only create confusion instead of assisting the memory."

71. We shall now proceed to apply the formulæ of Art. 62 to the solution of right-angled triangles. We shall assume that the given quantities are subject to the limitations which are stated in Arts. 22 and 23, that is, a given side must be less than the semicircumference of a great circle, and a given angle less than two right angles. There will be six cases to consider.

72. *Having given the hypotenuse c and an angle A.*

Here we have from (3), (5) and (2) of Art. 62,

$$\tan b = \tan c \cos A, \quad \cot B = \cos c \tan A, \quad \sin a = \sin c \sin A.$$

Thus b and B are determined immediately without ambiguity; and as a must be of the same affection as A (Art. 64), a also is determined without ambiguity.

It is obvious from the formulæ of solution, that in this case the triangle is always possible.

If c and A are both right angles, a is a right angle, and b and B are indeterminate.

73. *Having given a side b and the adjacent angle A.*

Here we have from (3), (4) and (6) of Art. 62,

$$\tan c = \frac{\tan b}{\cos A}, \quad \tan a = \tan A \sin b, \quad \cos B = \cos b \sin A.$$

Here c, a, B are determined without ambiguity, and the triangle is always possible.

74. *Having given the two sides a and b.*

Here we have from (1) and (4) of Art. 62,

$\cos c = \cos a \cos b$, $\cot A = \cot a \sin b$, $\cot B = \cot b \sin a$.

Here c, A, B are determined without ambiguity, and the triangle is always possible.

75. *Having given the hypotenuse c and a side a.*

Here we have from (1), (3) and (2) of Art. 62,

$$\cos b = \frac{\cos c}{\cos a}, \quad \cos B = \frac{\tan a}{\tan c}, \quad \sin A = \frac{\sin a}{\sin c}.$$

Here b, B, A are determined without ambiguity, since A must be of the same affection as a. It will be seen from these formulæ that there are limitations of the data in order to insure a possible triangle; in fact, c must lie between a and $\pi - a$ in order that the values found for $\cos b$, $\cos B$, and $\sin A$ may be numerically not greater than unity.

If c and a are right angles, A is a right angle, and b and B are indeterminate.

76. *Having given the two angles A and B.*

Here we have from (5) and (6) of Art. 62,

$$\cos c = \cot A \cot B, \quad \cos a = \frac{\cos A}{\sin B}, \quad \cos b = \frac{\cos B}{\sin A}.$$

Here $c,\ a,\ b$ are determined without ambiguity. There are limitations of the data in order to insure a possible triangle.

First suppose A less than $\dfrac{\pi}{2}$, then B must lie between $\dfrac{\pi}{2} - A$ and $\dfrac{\pi}{2} + A$; next suppose A greater than $\dfrac{\pi}{2}$, then B must lie between $\dfrac{\pi}{2} - (\pi - A)$ and $\dfrac{\pi}{2} + (\pi - A)$, that is, between $A - \dfrac{\pi}{2}$ and $\dfrac{3\pi}{2} - A$.

77. *Having given* a *side a and the opposite angle A.*

Here we have from (2), (4) and (6) of Art. 62,

$$\sin c = \frac{\sin a}{\sin A},\quad \sin b = \tan a \cot A,\quad \sin B = \frac{\sin A}{\cos a}.$$

Here there is an ambiguity, as the parts are determined from their sines. If $\sin a$ be less than $\sin A$, there are two values admissible for c; corresponding to each of these there will be *in general* only one admissible value of b, since we must have $\cos c = \cos a \cos b$, and only one admissible value of B, since we must have $\cos c = \cot A \cot B$. Thus if one triangle exists with the given parts, there will be *in general* two, and only two, triangles with the given parts. We say *in general* in the preceding sentences, because if $a = A$ there will be only *one* triangle, unless a and A are each right angles, and then b and B become indeterminate.

It is easy to see from a figure that the ambiguity must occur in general.

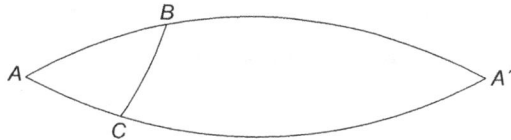

For, suppose *BAC* to be a triangle which satisfies the given conditions; produce *AB* and *AC* to meet again at *A'*; then the triangle *A'BC* also satisfies the given conditions, for it has a right angle at *C*, *BC* the given side, and *A' = A* the given angle.

If *a = A*, then the formulæ of solution shew that *c*, *b*, and *B* are right angles; in this case *A* is the pole of *BC*, and the triangle *A'BC* is symmetrically equal to the triangle *ABC* (Art. 57).

If *a* and *A* are both right angles, *B* is the pole of *AC*; *B* and *b* are then equal, but may have any value whatever.

There are limitations of the data in order to insure a possible triangle. *A* and *a* must have the same affection by Art. 64; hence the formulæ of solution shew that *a* must be less than *A* if both are acute, and greater than *A* if both are obtuse.

EXAMPLES

If *ABC* be a triangle in which the angle *C* is a right angle, prove the following relations contained in Examples 1 to 5.

1. $\sin^2 \dfrac{c}{2} = \sin^2 \dfrac{a}{2}\cos^2 \dfrac{b}{2} + \cos^2 \dfrac{a}{2}\sin^2 \dfrac{b}{2}.$

2. $\tan\dfrac{1}{2}(c+a)\tan\dfrac{1}{2}(c-a)=\tan^{2}\dfrac{b}{2}.$

3. $\sin(c-b)=\tan^{2}\dfrac{A}{2}\sin(c+b).$

4. $\sin a\tan\dfrac{1}{2}A-\sin b\tan\dfrac{1}{2}B=\sin(a-b).$

5. $\sin(c-a)=\sin b\cos a\tan\dfrac{1}{2}B,$

    $\sin(c-a)=\tan b\cos c\tan\dfrac{1}{2}B.$

6. If ABC be a spherical triangle, right-angled at C, and $\cos A = \cos^{2} a$, shew that if A be not a right angle $b+c=\frac{1}{2}\pi$ or $\dfrac{3}{2}\pi$, according as b and c are both less or both greater than $\dfrac{\pi}{2}$.

7. If $\alpha,\ \beta$ be the arcs drawn from the right angle respectively perpendicular to and bisecting the hypotenuse c, shew that

    $$\sin^{2}\dfrac{c}{2}\big(1+\sin^{2}\alpha\big)+\sin^{2}\beta.$$

8. In a triangle, if C be a right angle and D the middle point of AB, shew that

    $$4\cos^{2}\dfrac{c}{2}\sin^{2}CD=\sin^{2}a+\sin^{2}b.$$

9. In a right-angled triangle, if δ be the length of the arc drawn from C perpendicular to the hypotenuse AB, shew that

$$\cot \delta = \sqrt{(\cot^2 a + \cot^2 b)}.$$

10. OAA_1 is a spherical triangle right-angled at A_1 and acute-angled at A; the arc A_1A_2 of a great circle is drawn perpendicular to OA, then A_2A_3 is drawn perpendicular to OA_1, and so on: shew that A_nA_{n+1} vanishes when n becomes infinite; and find the value of $\cos AA_1 \cos A_1A_2 \cos A_2A_3 ...$ to infinity.

11. ABC is a right-angled spherical triangle, A not being the right angle: shew that if $A = a$, then c and b are quadrants.

12. If δ be the length of the arc drawn from C perpendicular to AB in *any* triangle, shew that

$$\cos \delta = \operatorname{cosec} c \, (\cos^2 a + \cos^2 b - 2 \cos a \cos b \cos c)^{\frac{1}{2}}.$$

13. ABC is a great circle of a sphere; AA', BB', CC', are arcs of great circles drawn at right angles to ABC and reckoned positive when they lie on the same side of it: shew that the condition of A', B', C' lying in a great circle is

$\tan AA' \sin BC + \tan BB' \sin CA + \tan CC' \sin AB = 0.$

14. Perpendiculars are drawn from the angles A, B, C of any triangle meeting the opposite sides at D, E, F respectively: shew that

$\tan BD \tan CE \tan AF = \tan DC \tan EA \tan FB.$

15. *Ox, Oy* are two great circles of a sphere at right angles to each other, *P* is any point in *AB* another great circle. $OC = p$ is the arc perpendicular to *AB* from *O*, making the angle $COx = a$ with *Ox*. *PM, PN* are arcs perpendicular to *Ox, Oy* respectively: shew that if $OM = x$ and $ON = y$,

$$\cos a \tan x + \sin a \tan y = \tan p.$$

16. The position of a point on a sphere, with reference to two great circles at right angles to each other as axes, is determined by the portions θ, ϕ of these circles cut off by great circles through the point, and through two points on the axes, each $\dfrac{\pi}{2}$ from their point of intersection: shew that if the three points $(\theta, \phi), (\theta, \phi'), (\theta'', \phi'')$ lie on the same great circle

$$\tan \phi(\tan \theta' - \tan \theta'') + \tan \phi(\tan \theta'' - \tan \theta)$$
$$+ \tan \phi''(\tan \theta - \tan \theta') = 0.$$

17. If a point on a sphere be referred to two great circles at right angles to each other as axes, by means of the portions of these axes cut off by great circles drawn through the point and two points on the axes each 90° from their intersection, shew that the equation to a great circle is

$$\tan \theta \cot \alpha + \tan \phi \cot \beta = 1.$$

18. In a spherical triangle, if $A = \dfrac{\pi}{5}, B = \dfrac{\pi}{3}$, and, $C = \dfrac{\pi}{2}$, shew that $a + b + c = \dfrac{\pi}{2}$.

SOLUTION OF OBLIQUE-ANGLED TRIANGLES

78. The solution of oblique-angled triangles may be made in some cases to depend immediately on the solution of right-angled triangles; we will indicate these cases before considering the subject generally.

1. Suppose a triangle to have one of its given sides equal to a *quadrant*. In this case the polar triangle has its corresponding angle a right angle; the polar triangle can therefore be solved by the rules of the preceding Chapter, and thus the elements of the primitive triangle become known.

2. Suppose among the given elements of a triangle there are two *equal sides* or two *equal angles*. By drawing an arc from the vertex to the middle point of the base, the triangle is divided into two equal *right-angled* triangles; by the solution of one of these right-angled triangles the required elements can be found.

3. Suppose among the given elements of a triangle there are two sides, one of which is the supplement of the other, or two angles, one of which is the supplement of the other. Suppose, for example, that $b + c = \pi$, or else that $B + C = \pi$; produce BA and BC to meet at B' (see the first figure to Art. 38); then the triangle $B'AC$ has two equal sides given, or else two equal angles given; and by the preceding case the solution of it can be made to depend on the solution of a right-angled triangle.

79. We now proceed to the solution of oblique-angled triangles in general. There will be six cases to consider.

80. *Having given the three sides.*

Here we have $\cos A = \dfrac{\cos a - \cos b \cos c}{\sin b \sin c}$, and similar formulæ for $\cos B$ and $\cos C$. Or if we wish to use formulæ suited to logarithms, we may take the formula for the sine, cosine, or tangent of half an angle given in Art. 45. In selecting a formula, attention should be paid to the remarks in *Plane Trigonometry*, Chapter 12 towards the end.

81. *Having given the three angles.*

Here we have $\cos a = \dfrac{\cos A + \cos B \cos C}{\sin B \sin C}$, and similar formulæ for $\cos b$ and $\cos c$. Or if we wish to use formulæ suited to logarithms, we may take the formula for the sine, cosine, or tangent of half a side given in Art. 49.

There is no ambiguity in the two preceding cases; the triangles however may be impossible with the given elements.

82. *Having given two sides and the included angle* (a, C, b).

By Napier's analogies

$$\tan\frac{1}{2}(A+B) = \frac{\cos\frac{1}{2}(a-b)}{\cos\frac{1}{2}(a+b)}\cot\frac{1}{2}C,$$

$$\tan\frac{1}{2}(A-B) = \frac{\sin\frac{1}{2}(a-b)}{\sin\frac{1}{2}(a+b)}\cot\frac{1}{2}C;$$

these determine $\frac{1}{2}(A+b)$ and $\frac{1}{2}(A-B)$, and thence A and B.

Then c may be found from the formula $\sin c = \dfrac{\sin a \sin C}{\sin A}$; in this case, since c is found from its sine, it may be uncertain which of two values is to be given to it; the point may be sometimes settled by observing that the greater side of a triangle is opposite to the greater angle. Or we may determine c from equation (1) of Art. 54, which is free from ambiguity.

Or we may determine c, without previously determining A and B, from the formula $\cos c = \cos a \cos b + \sin a \sin b \cos C$; this is free from ambiguity. This formula may be adapted to logarithms thus:

$$\cos c = \cos b \,(\cos a + \sin a \tan b \cos C);$$

assume $\tan \theta = \tan b \cos C$; then

$$\cos c = \cos b(\cos a + \sin a \tan \theta) = \frac{\cos b \cos(a - \theta)}{\cos \theta};$$

this is adapted to logarithms.

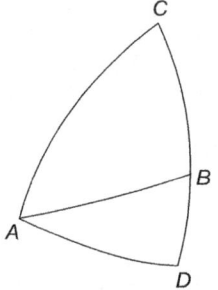 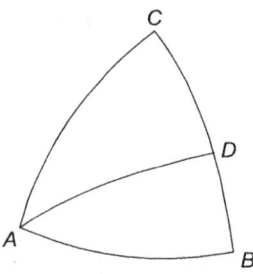

Or we may treat this case conveniently by resolving the triangle into the sum or difference of two right-angled triangles. From A draw the arc AD perpendicular to CB or CB produced; then, by Art. 62, $\tan CD = \tan b \cos C$, and this determines CD, and then DB is known. Again, by Art. 62,

$$\cos c = \cos AD \cos DB = \cos DB \frac{\cos b}{\cos CD};$$

this finds c. It is obvious that CD is what was denoted by θ in the former part of the Article.

By Art. 62,

$\tan AD = \tan C \sin CD$, and $\tan AD = \tan ABD \sin DB$;

thus $\tan ABD \sin DB = \tan C \sin \theta,$

where $DB = a - \theta$ or $\theta - a$, according as D is on CB or CB produced, and ABD is either B or the supplement of B; this formula enables us to find B independently of A.

Thus, in the present case, there is no real ambiguity, and the triangle is always possible.

83. *Having given two angles and the included side* (A, c, B).

By Napier's analogies,

$$\tan \frac{1}{2}(a+b) = \frac{\cos \frac{1}{2}(A-B)}{\cos \frac{1}{2}(A+B)} \tan \frac{1}{2}c,$$

$$\tan \frac{1}{2}(a-b) = \frac{\sin \frac{1}{2}(A-B)}{\sin \frac{1}{2}(A+B)} \tan \frac{1}{2}c;$$

these determine $\frac{1}{2}(a+b)$ and $\frac{1}{2}(a-b)$ and thence a and b.

Then C may be found from the formula $\sin C = \dfrac{\sin A \sin c}{\sin a}$; in this case, since C is found from its sine, it may be uncertain which of two values is to be given to it; the point may be sometimes settled by observing that the greater angle of a triangle is opposite to the greater side. Or we may determine C from equation (3) of Art. 54, which is free from ambiguity.

Or we may determine C without previously determining a and b from the formula $\cos C = -\cos A \cos B + \sin A \sin B \cos c$. This formula may be adapted to logarithms, thus:

$$\cos C = \cos B(-\cos A + \sin A \tan B \cos c);$$

assume $\cot \phi = \tan B \cos c$; then

$$\cos C = \cos B(-\cos A + \cot \phi \sin A) = \frac{\cos B \sin(A - \phi)}{\sin \phi};$$

this is adapted to logarithms.

Or we may treat this case conveniently by resolving the triangle into the sum or difference of two right-angled triangles. From A draw the arc AD perpendicular to CB (see the right-hand figure of Art. 82); then, by Art. 62, $\cos c = \cot B \cot DAB$, and this determines DAB, and then CAD is known. Again, by Art. 62,

$$\cos AD \sin CAD = \cos C, \text{ and } \cos AD \sin BAD = \cos B;$$

therefore $\dfrac{\cos C}{\sin CAD} = \dfrac{\cos B}{\sin BAD}$; this finds C.

It is obvious that DAB is what was denoted by ϕ in the former part of the Article.

By Art. 62,

$$\tan AD = \tan AC \cos CAD, \text{ and } \tan AD = \tan AB \cos BAD;$$

thus $\tan b \cos CAD = \tan c \cos \phi$,

where $CAD = A - \phi$; this formula enables us to find b independently of a.

Similarly we may proceed when the perpendicular AD falls on CB *produced*; (see the left-hand figure of Art. 82).

Thus, in the present case, there is no real ambiguity; moreover the triangle is always possible.

84. *Having given two sides and the angle opposite one of them* (*a*, *b*, *A*).

The angle *B* may be found from the formula

$$\sin B = \frac{\sin b}{\sin a} \sin A;$$

and then *C* and *c* may be found from Napier's analogies,

$$\tan \frac{1}{2} C = \frac{\cos \frac{1}{2}(a-b)}{\cos \frac{1}{2}(a+b)} \cot \frac{1}{2}(A+B),$$

$$\tan \frac{1}{2} c = \frac{\cos \frac{1}{2}(A+B)}{\cos \frac{1}{2}(A-B)} \tan \frac{1}{2}(a+b).$$

In this case, since *B* is found from its sine, there will sometimes be two solutions; and sometimes there will be no solution at all, namely, when the value found for sin *B* is greater than unity. We will presently return to this point. (See Art. 86.)

We may also determine *C* and c independently of *B* by formulæ adapted to logarithms. For, by Art. 44,

$$\cot a \sin b = \cos b \cos C + \sin C \cot A$$

$$= \cos b \left(\cos C + \frac{\cot A}{\cos b} \sin C \right);$$

assume $\qquad\qquad \tan\phi = \dfrac{\cot A}{\cos b}$; thus

$$\cot a \sin b = \cos b\left(\cos C + \tan\phi \sin C\right) = \frac{\cos b \cos\left(C-\phi\right)}{\cos\phi};$$

therefore $\cos(C-\phi) = \cos\phi\cot a\tan b$;

from this equation $C-\phi$ is to be found, and then C. The ambiguity still exists; for if the last equation leads to $C-\phi = a$, it will be satisfied also by $\phi - C = a$; so that we have two admissible values for C, if $\phi + a$ is less than π, and $\phi - a$ is positive.

And

$$\cos a = \cos b \cos c + \sin b \sin c \cos A$$

$$= \cos b(\cos c + \sin c \tan b \cos A);$$

assume $\tan\theta = \tan b\cos A$; thus

$$\cos a = \cos b(\cos c + \sin c \tan\theta) = \frac{\cos b \cos(c-\theta)}{\cos\theta};$$

therefore $\qquad \cos(c-\theta) = \dfrac{\cos a \cos\theta}{\cos b}$;

from this equation $c-\theta$ is to be found, and then c; and there may be an ambiguity as before.

Or we may treat this case conveniently by resolving the triangle into the sum or difference of two right-angled triangles.

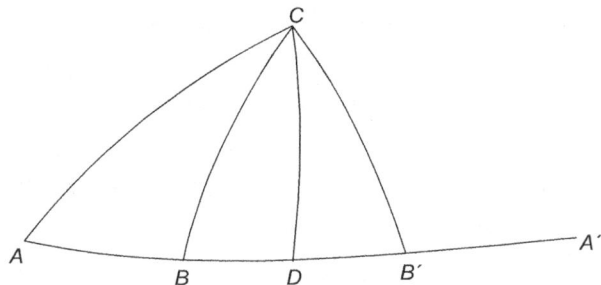

Let $CA = b$, and let $CAE =$ the given angle A; from C draw CD perpendicular to AE, and let CB and $CB' = a$; thus the figure shews that there may be two triangles which have the given elements. Then, by Art. 62, $\cos b = \cot A \cot ACD$; this finds ACD. Again, by Art. 62,

$$\tan CD = \tan AC \cos ACD,$$

and $\tan CD = \tan CB \cos BCD$, or $\tan CB' \cos B'CD$,

therefore $\tan AC \cos ACD = \tan CB \cos BCD$, or $\tan CB'$ $\cos B'CD$; this finds BCD or $B'CD$.

It is obvious that ACD is what was denoted by ϕ in the former part of the Article.

Also, by Art. 62, $\tan AD = \tan AC \cos A$; this finds AD. Then

$$\cos AC = \cos CD \cos AD,$$

$$\cos CB = \cos CD \cos BD,$$

$$\text{or } \cos CB' = \cos CD \cos B'D;$$

therefore $\quad \dfrac{\cos AC}{\cos AD} = \dfrac{\cos CB}{\cos BD}$ or $\dfrac{\cos CB'}{\cos B'D}$;

this finds BD or $B'D$.

It is obvious that AD is what was denoted by θ in the former part of the Article.

85. *Having given two angles and the side opposite one of them (A, B, a).*

This case is analogous to that immediately preceding, and gives rise to the same ambiguities. The side b may be found from the formula

$$\sin b = \frac{\sin B \sin a}{\sin A};$$

and then C and c may be found from Napier's analogies,

$$\tan\frac{1}{2}C = \frac{\cos\frac{1}{2}(a-b)}{\cos\frac{1}{2}(a+b)}\cot\frac{1}{2}(A+B),$$

$$\tan\frac{1}{2}c = \frac{\cos\frac{1}{2}(A+B)}{\cos\frac{1}{2}(A-B)}\tan\frac{1}{2}(a+b),$$

We may also determine C and c independently of b by formulæ adapted to logarithms. For

$$\cos A = -\cos B \cos C + \sin B \sin C \cos a$$

$$= \cos B(-\cos C + \tan B \sin C \cos a),$$

assume cot ϕ = tan B cos a; thus

$$\cos A = \cos B\left(-\cos C + \sin C \cot \phi\right) = \frac{\cos B \sin\left(C - \phi\right)}{\sin \phi};$$

therefore $\qquad \sin\left(C - \phi\right) = \frac{\cos A \sin \phi}{\cos B};$

from this equation $C - \phi$ is to be found and then C. Since $C - \phi$ is found from its sine there may be an ambiguity. Again, by Art. 44,

$$\cot A \sin B = \cot a \sin c - \cos c \cos B$$

$$= \cos B\left(-\cos c + \frac{\cot a \sin c}{\cos B}\right).$$

assume $\qquad \cot \theta = \dfrac{\cot a}{\cos B}$; then

$$\cot A \sin B = \cos B\left(-\cos c + \sin c \cot \theta\right) = \frac{\cos B \sin\left(c - \theta\right)}{\sin \theta};$$

therefore $\qquad \sin(c - \theta) = \cot A \tan B \sin \theta;$

from this equation $c - \theta$ is to be found, and then c. Since $c - \theta$ is found from its sine there may be an ambiguity. As before, it may be shewn that these results agree with those obtained by resolving the triangle into two right-angled triangles; for if in the triangle ACB' the arc CD be drawn perpendicular to AB', then $B'CD$ will = ϕ, and $B'D = \theta$.

86. We now return to the consideration of the ambiguity which may occur in the case of Art. 84, when two sides are given and the angle opposite one of them. The discussion is somewhat tedious from its length, but presents no difficulty.

Before considering the problem generally, we will take the particular case in which $a = b$; then A must $= B$. The first and third of Napier's analogies give

$$\cot \frac{1}{2}C = \tan A \cos a, \quad \tan \frac{1}{2}c = \tan a \cos A;$$

now $\cot \frac{1}{2}C$ and $\tan \frac{1}{2}C$ must both be *positive*, so that A and a must be of same affection. Hence, when $a = b$, there will be no solution at all, unless A and a are of the same affection, and then there will be only one solution; except when A and a are both right angles, and then $\cot \frac{1}{2}C$ and $\tan \frac{1}{2}c$ are indeterminate, and there is an infinite number of solutions.

We now proceed to the general discussion.

If $\sin b \sin A$ be greater than $\sin a$, there is no triangle which satisfies the given conditions; if $\sin b \sin A$ is *not* greater than $\sin a$, the equation $\sin B = \dfrac{\sin b \sin A}{\sin a}$ furnishes two values of B, which we will denote by β and β', so that $\beta' = \pi - \beta$; we will suppose that β is the one which is not greater than the other.

Now, in order that these values of B may be admissible, it is necessary and sufficient that the values of $\cot \frac{1}{2} C$ and of $\tan \frac{1}{2} c$ should both be positive, that is, $A - B$ and $a - b$ must have the same sign by the second and fourth of Napier's analogies. We have therefore to compare the sign of $A - \beta$ and the sign of $A - \beta'$ with that of $a - b$.

We will suppose that A is less than a right angle, and separate the corresponding discussion into three cases.

I. Let b be less than $\frac{\pi}{2}$.

1. Let a be less than b; the formula $\sin B = \dfrac{\sin b}{\sin a} \sin A$ make β greater than A, and *a fortiori* β' greater than A. Hence there are two solutions.

2. Let a be equal to b; then there is one solution, as previously shewn.

3. Let a be greater than b; we may have then $a + b$ less than π or equal to π or greater than π. If $a + b$ is less than π, then $\sin a$ is greater than $\sin b$; thus β is less than A and therefore admissible, and β' is greater than A and inadmissible. Hence there is one solution. If $a + b$ is equal to π, then β is equal to A and β' greater than A and both and inadmissible. If $a + b$ is greater than π, then $\sin a$ is less than $\sin b$, and β and β' are both greater than A, and both inadmissible. Hence there is no solution.

II.   Let b be equal to $\dfrac{\pi}{2}$.

1. Let a be less than b; then β and β' are both greater than A, and both admissible. Hence there are two solutions.

2. Let a be equal to b; then there is no solution, as previously shewn.

3. Let a be greater than b; then $\sin a$ is less than $\sin b$, and β and β' are both greater than A, and inadmissible. Hence there is no solution.

III.   Let b be greater than $\dfrac{\pi}{2}$.

1. Let a be less than b; we may have then $a + b$ less than π or equal to π or greater than π. If $a + b$ is less than π, then $\sin a$ is less than $\sin b$, and β and β' are both greater than A and both admissible. Hence there are two solutions. If $a + b$ is equal to π, then β is equal to A and inadmissible, and β' is greater than A and inadmissible. Hence there is one solution. If $a + b$ is greater than π, then $\sin a$ is greater than $\sin b$; β is less than A and admissible, and β' is greater than A and admissible. Hence there is one solution.

2. Let a be equal to b; then there is no solution, as previously shewn.

3. Let a be greater than b; then $\sin a$ is less than $\sin b$, and β and β' are both greater than A and both inadmissible. Hence there is no solution.

We have then the following results when *A is less than a right angle.*

$$b < \frac{\pi}{2} \begin{cases} a < b\dots\dots\dots\dots\dots\text{two solutions,} \\ a = b\dots\dots\dots\dots\dots\text{one solution,} \\ a > b \text{ and } a + b < \pi\dots\dots\text{one solution,} \\ a > b \text{ and } a + b = \pi \text{ or} > \pi\dots\dots\text{no solution.} \end{cases}$$

$$b = \frac{\pi}{2} \begin{cases} a < b\dots\dots\dots\dots\dots\text{two solutions,} \\ a = b \text{ or } a > b\dots\dots\dots\dots\text{no solution.} \end{cases}$$

$$b > \frac{\pi}{2} \begin{cases} a < b \text{ and } a + b < \pi\dots\dots\dots\text{two solutions,} \\ a < b \text{ and } a + b = \pi \text{ or} > \pi\dots\dots\text{one solution,} \\ a = b \text{ or} > b\dots\dots\dots\dots\text{no solution.} \end{cases}$$

It must be remembered, however, that in the cases in which two solutions are indicated, there will be no solution at all if sin *a* be less than sin *b* sin *A*.

In the same manner the cases in which *A* is equal to a right angle or greater than a right angle may be discussed, and the following results obtained.

When A is equal to a right angle,

$$b < \frac{\pi}{2} \begin{cases} a < b \text{ or } a = b\dots\dots\dots\dots\text{no solution,} \\ a > b \text{ and } a + b < \pi\dots\dots\dots\text{one solution,} \\ a > b \text{ and } a + b = \pi \text{ or} > \pi\dots\dots\text{no solution.} \end{cases}$$

$$b = \frac{\pi}{2} \begin{cases} a < b \text{ or } a > b \dots\dots\dots\dots\dots\dots \text{no solution,} \\ a = b \dots\dots\dots\dots \text{infinite number of solutions.} \end{cases}$$

$$b > \frac{\pi}{2} \begin{cases} a < b \text{ and } a + b > \pi \dots\dots\dots\dots\dots\dots \text{one solution,} \\ a < b \text{ and } a + b = \pi \text{ or } < \pi \dots\dots\dots\dots \text{no solution,} \\ a = b \text{ or } a > b \dots\dots\dots\dots\dots\dots\dots\dots \text{no solution.} \end{cases}$$

When A is greater than a right angle,

$$b < \frac{\pi}{2} \begin{cases} a < b \text{ or } a = b \dots\dots\dots\dots\dots\dots\dots \text{no solution,} \\ a > b \text{ and } a + b = \pi \text{ or } < \pi \dots\dots\dots \text{one solution,} \\ a > b \text{ and } a + b > \pi \dots\dots\dots\dots\dots \text{two solution.} \end{cases}$$

$$b = \frac{\pi}{2} \begin{cases} a < b \text{ or } a = b \dots\dots\dots\dots\dots\dots\dots \text{no solution,} \\ a > b \dots\dots\dots\dots\dots\dots\dots\dots\dots\dots \text{two solutions.} \end{cases}$$

$$b > \frac{\pi}{2} \begin{cases} a < b \text{ and } a + b > \pi \dots\dots\dots\dots\dots\dots \text{one solution,} \\ a < b \text{ and } a + b = \pi \text{ or } < \pi \dots\dots\dots\dots \text{no solution,} \\ a = b \dots\dots\dots\dots\dots\dots\dots\dots\dots\dots\dots\dots \text{one solution,} \\ a > b \dots\dots\dots\dots\dots\dots\dots\dots\dots\dots\dots \text{two solutions.} \end{cases}$$

As before in the cases in which two solutions are indicated, there will be no solution at all if $\sin a$ be less than $\sin b \sin A$.

It will be seen from the above investigations that if a lies between b and $\pi - b$, there will be one solution; if a does not lie between b and $\pi - b$ either there are two solutions or there is no solution; this enunciation is not meant to include the cases in which $a = b$ or $= \pi - b$.

87. The results of the preceding Article may be illustrated by a figure.

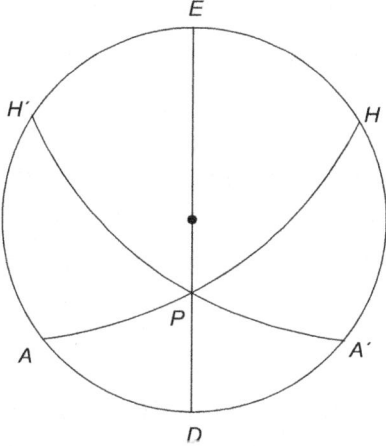

Let $ADA'E$ be a great circle; suppose PA and PA' the projections on the plane of this circle of arcs which are each equal to b and inclined at an angle A to ADA'; let PD and PE be the projections of the least and greatest distances of P from the great circle (see Art. 59). Thus the figure supposes A and b each less than $\dfrac{\pi}{2}$.

If a be less than the arc which is represented by PD there is no triangle; if a be between PD and PA in magnitude, there are two triangles, since B will fall on ADA', and we have two triangles BPA and BPA'; if a be between PA and PH there will be only one triangle, as B will fall on $A'H$ or AH', and the triangle will be either APB with B between A' and H, or else $A'PB$ with B between A and H'; but these two triangles are symmetrically equal (Art. 57); if a be greater than PH there will be no triangle. The figure will easily serve for all the cases;

thus if A is greater than $\dfrac{\pi}{2}$, we can suppose *PAE* and *PA'E*

to be equal to A; if b is greater than $\dfrac{\pi}{2}$, we can take *PH* and

PH' to represent b.

88. The ambiguities which occur in the last case in the solution of oblique-angled triangles (Art. 85) may be discussed in the same manner as those in Art. 86; or, by means of the polar triangle, the last case may be deduced from that of Art. 86.

EXAMPLES

1. The sides of a triangle are $105°$, $90°$, and $75°$ respectively: find the sines of all the angles.

2. Shew that $\tan\dfrac{1}{2}A\tan\dfrac{1}{2}B = \dfrac{\sin(s-c)}{\sin s}$. Solve a triangle when a side, an adjacent angle, and the sum of the other two sides are given.

3. Solve a triangle having given a side, an adjacent angle, and the sum of ther other two angles.

4. A triangle has the sum of two sides equal to a semicircumference: find the arc joining the vertex with the middle of the base.

5. If a, b, c are known, c being a *quadrant*, determine the angles: shew also that if δ be the perpendicular on c from the opposite angle, $\cos^2\delta = \cos^2 a + \cos^2 b$.

6. If one side of a spherical triangle be divided into four equal parts, and θ_1, θ_2, θ_3, θ_4, be the angles subtended at the opposite angle by the parts taken in order, shew that

$$\sin(\theta_1 + \theta_2)\sin\theta_2\sin\theta_4 = \sin(\theta_3 + \theta_4)\sin\theta_1\sin\theta_3.$$

7. In a spherical triangle if $A = B = 2C$, shew that

$$8\sin\left(a + \frac{c}{2}\right)\sin^2\frac{c}{2}\cos\frac{c}{2} = \sin^3 a.$$

8. In a spherical triangle if $A = B = 2C$, shew that

$$8\sin^2\frac{C}{2}\left(\cos s + \sin\frac{C}{2}\right)\frac{\cos\frac{c}{2}}{\cos a} = 1.$$

9. If the equal sides of an isosceles triangle ABC be bisected by an arc DE, and BC be the base, shew that

$$\sin\frac{DE}{2} = \frac{1}{2}\sin\frac{BC}{2}\sec\frac{AC}{2}.$$

10. If c_1, c_2 be the two values of the third side when A, a, b are given and the triangle is ambiguous, shew that

$$\tan\frac{c_1}{2}\tan\frac{c_2}{2} = \tan\frac{1}{2}(b - a)\tan\frac{1}{2}(b + a).$$

CIRCUMSCRIBED AND INSCRIBED CIRCLES

89. *To find the angular radius of the small circle inscribed in a given triangle.*

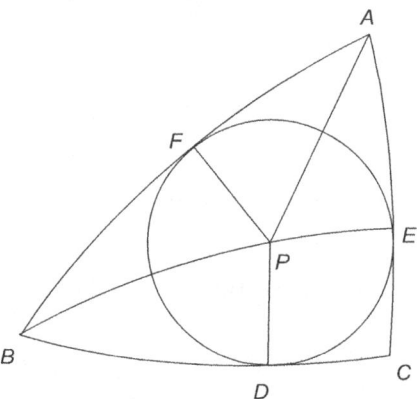

Let *ABC* be the triangle; bisect the angles *A* and *B* by arcs meeting at *P*; from *P* draw *PD*, *PE*, *PF* perpendicular to the sides. Then it may be shewn that *PD*, *PE*, *PF* are all equal; also that $AE = AF$, $BF = BD$, $CD = CE$.

Hence $BC + AF$ = half the sum of the sides = s; therefore $AF = s - a$. Let $PF = r$.

Now $\tan PF = \tan PAF \sin AF$ (Art. 62);

thus $\tan r = \tan \dfrac{A}{2} \sin(s-a).$ (1)

The value of $\tan r$ may be expressed in various forms; thus from Art. 45, we obtain

$$\tan \frac{A}{2} = \sqrt{\frac{\sin(s-b)\sin(s-c)}{\sin s \, \sin(s-a)}};$$

substitute this value in (1), thus

$$\tan r = \sqrt{\left\{ \frac{\sin(s-a)\sin(s-b)\sin(s-c)}{\sin s} \right\}} = \frac{n}{\sin s}\text{(Art. 46).(2)}$$

Again

$$\sin(s-a) = \sin\frac{1}{2}(b+c) - \frac{1}{2}a$$

$$= \sin\frac{1}{2}(b+c)\cos\frac{1}{2}a - \cos\frac{1}{2}(b+c)\sin\frac{1}{2}a$$

$$= \frac{\sin\frac{1}{2}a\cos\frac{1}{2}a}{\sin\frac{1}{2}A}\left\{ \cos\frac{1}{2}(B-C) - \cos\frac{1}{2}(B+C) \right\},$$

(Art.54)

$$= \frac{\sin a \sin\frac{1}{2}B \sin\frac{1}{2}C}{\sin\frac{1}{2}A};$$

therefore from (1) $\tan r = \dfrac{\sin \frac{1}{2} B \sin \frac{1}{2} C}{\cos \frac{1}{2} A} \sin a;$ (3)

hence, by Art. 51,

$$\tan r = \sqrt{\dfrac{\sqrt{\{-\cos S \cos(S - A) \cos(S - B) \cos(S - C)\}}}{2 \cos \frac{1}{2} A \cos \frac{1}{2} B \cos \frac{1}{2} C}}$$

$$= \dfrac{N}{2 \cos \frac{1}{2} A \cos \frac{1}{2} B \cos \frac{1}{2} C}. \qquad (4)$$

It may be shewn by common trigonometrical formulæ that

$$4 \cos \tfrac{1}{2} A \cos \tfrac{1}{2} B \cos \tfrac{1}{2} C = \cos S + \cos(S - A)$$
$$+ \cos(S - B) + \cos(S - C)$$

hence we have from (4)

$$\cot r = \dfrac{1}{2N} \{\cos S + \cos(S - A) + \cos(S - B) + \cos(S - C)\}. (5)$$

90. *To find the angular radius of the small circle described so as to touch one side of a given triangle, and the other sides produced.*

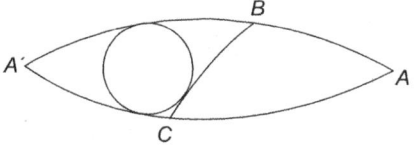

Let *ABC* be the triangle; and suppose we require the radius of the small circle which touches *BC*, and *AB* and *AC* produced. Produce *AB* and *AC* to meet at *A′*; then we require the radius of the small *circle inscribed in A'BC*, and the sides of *A'BC* are a, $\pi - b$, $\pi - c$ respectively. Hence if r_1 be the required radius, and s denote as usual $\frac{1}{2}(a+b+c)$ we have from Art. 89,

$$\tan r_1 = \tan \frac{A}{2} \sin s. \tag{1}$$

From this result we may derive other equivalent forms as in the preceding Article; or we may make use of those forms immediately, observing that the angles of the triangle *A'BC* are A, $\pi - B$, $\pi - C$ respectively. Hence s being $\frac{1}{2}(a+b+c)$ and S being $\frac{1}{2}(A+B+C)$ we shall obtain

$$\tan r_1 = \sqrt{\left\{ \frac{\sin s \sin(s-b)\sin(s-c)}{\sin(s-a)} \right\}} = \frac{n}{\sin(s-a)}, \tag{2}$$

$$\tan r_1 = \frac{\cos \frac{1}{2} B \cos \frac{1}{2} C}{\cos \frac{1}{2} A} \sin a, \tag{3}$$

$$\tan r_1 = \sqrt{\frac{\{-\cos S \cos(S-A)\cos(S-B)\cos(S-C)\}}{2\cos \frac{1}{2} A \sin \frac{1}{2} B \sin \frac{1}{2} C}} \tag{4}$$

$$= \frac{N}{2\cos \frac{1}{2} A \sin \frac{1}{2} B \sin \frac{1}{2} C},$$

$$\cot r_1 = \frac{1}{2N}\{-c\cos S - \cos(S-A) \\ + \cos(S-B) + \cos(S-C)\}. \tag{5}$$

These results may also be found independently by bisecting two of the angles of the triangle $A'BC$, so as to determine the pole of the small circle, and proceeding as in Art. 89.

91. A circle which touches one side of a triangle and the other sides produced is called an *escribed circle*; thus there are three escribed circles belonging to a given triangle. We may denote the radii of the escribed circles which touch CA and AB respectively by r_2 and r_3, and values of $\tan r_2$ and $\tan r_3$ may be found from what has been already given with respect to $\tan r_1$ by appropriate changes in the letters which denote the sides and angles.

In the preceding Article a triangle $A'BC$ was formed by producing AB and AC to meet again at A'; similarly another triangle may be formed by producing BC and BA to meet again, and another by producing CA and CB to meet again. The original triangle ABC and the three formed from it have been called *associated triangles*, ABC being the fundamental triangle. Thus the inscribed and escribed circles of a given triangle are the same as the circles inscribed in the system of associated triangles of which the given triangle is the fundamental triangle.

92. *To find the angular radius of the small circle described about a given triangle.*

Let ABC be the given triangle; bisect the sides CB, CA at D and E respectively, and draw from D and E arcs at right angles to CB and CA respectively, and let P be the intersection of these arcs.

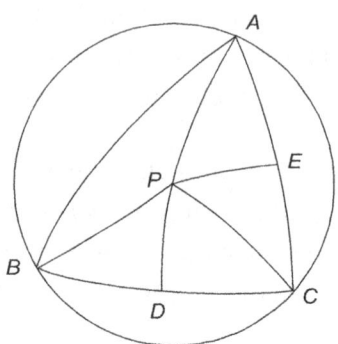

Then *P* will be the pole of the small circle described about *ABC*. For draw *PA*, *PB*, *PC*; then from the right-angled triangles *PCD* and *PBD* it follows that *PB* = *PC*; and from the right-angled triangles *PCE* and *PAE* it follows that *PA* = *PC*; hence *PA* = *PB* = *PC*. Also the angle *P AB* = the angle *P BA*, the angle *PBC* = the angle *PCB*, and the angle *PCA* = the angle *PAC*; therefore

$$PCB + A = \frac{1}{2}(A + B + C), \text{ and } PCB = S - A.$$

Let *PC* = *R*.

Now tan *CD* = tan *CP* cos *PCD*, (Art. 62,)

thus $$\tan \frac{1}{2}a = \tan R \cos(S - A),$$

therefore $$\tan R = \frac{\tan \frac{1}{2}a}{\cos(S - A)}. \qquad (1)$$

The value of tan R may be expressed in various forms; thus if we substitute for $\tan \dfrac{a}{2}$ from Art. 49, we obtain

$$\tan R = \sqrt{\left\{ \frac{-\cos S}{\cos(S-A)\cos(S-B)\cos(S-C)} \right\}} = \frac{\cos S}{N}. \quad (2)$$

Again

$$\cos(S-A) = \cos\left\{ \frac{1}{2}(B+C) - \frac{1}{2}A \right\}$$

$$= \cos\frac{1}{2}(B+C)\cos\frac{1}{2}A + \sin\frac{1}{2}(B+C)\sin\frac{1}{2}A$$

$$= \frac{\sin\frac{1}{2}A\cos\frac{1}{2}A}{\cos\frac{1}{2}a}\left\{ \cos\frac{1}{2}(b+c) + \cos\frac{1}{2}(b-c) \right\},$$

(Art. 54,)

$$= \frac{\sin A}{\cos\frac{1}{2}a}\cos\frac{1}{2}b\cos\frac{1}{2}c;$$

therefore from (1)

$$\tan R = \frac{\sin\frac{1}{2}a}{\sin A\cos\frac{1}{2}b\cos\frac{1}{2}c}. \quad (3)$$

Substitute in the last expression the value of $\sin A$ from Art. 46; thus

$$\tan R = \frac{2\sin\frac{1}{2}a\sin\frac{1}{2}b\sin\frac{1}{2}c}{\sqrt{\{\sin s\sin(s-a)\sin(s-b)\sin(s-c)\}}}$$

$$= \frac{2\sin\frac{1}{2}a\sin\frac{1}{2}b\sin\frac{1}{2}c}{n}. \quad (4)$$

It may be shewn, by common trigonometrical formulæ that

$$4\sin\frac{1}{2}a\sin\frac{1}{2}b\sin\frac{1}{2}c = \sin(s-a)+\sin(s-b)$$
$$+\sin(s-c)-\sin s;$$

hence we have from (4)

$$\tan R = \frac{1}{2n}\{\sin(s-a)+\sin(s-b)+\sin(s-c)-\sin s\}. \quad (5)$$

93. *To find the angular radii of the small circles described round the triangles associated with a given fundamental triangle.*

Let R_1 denote the radius of the circle described round the triangle formed by producing AB and AC to meet again at A'; similarly let R_2 and R_3 denote the radii of the circles described round the other two triangles which are similarly formed. Then we may deduce expressions for $\tan R_1$, $\tan R_2$, and $\tan R_3$ from those found in Art. 92 for $\tan R$. The sides of the triangle $A'BC$ are a, $\pi - b$, $\pi - c$, and its angles are A, $\pi - B$, $\pi - C$; hence if $s = \frac{1}{2}(a+b+c)$ and $S = \frac{1}{2}(A+B+C)$ we shall obtain from Art. 92

$$\tan R_1 = \frac{\tan\frac{1}{2}a}{-\cos S}, \quad (1)$$

$$\tan R_1 = \sqrt{\left\{\frac{\cos(S-A)}{-\cos S\cos(S-B)\cos(S-C)}\right\}} = \frac{\cos(S-A)}{N}, \quad (2)$$

$$\tan R_1 = \frac{\sin \frac{1}{2} a}{\sin A \sin \frac{1}{2} b \sin \frac{1}{2} c}, \tag{3}$$

$$\tan R_1 = \frac{2 \sin \frac{1}{2} a \cos \frac{1}{2} b \cos \frac{1}{2} c}{\sqrt{\{\sin s \sin(s-a) \sin(s-b) \sin(s-c)\}}}, \tag{4}$$

$$\tan R_1 = \frac{1}{2n} \{\sin s - \sin(s-a) + \sin(s-b) + \sin(s-c)\}. \tag{5}$$

Similarly we may find expressions for $\tan R_2$ and $\tan R_3$.

94. Many examples may be proposed involving properties of the circles inscribed in and described about the associated triangles. We will give one that will be of use hereafter.

To prove that

$$(\cot r + \tan R)^2 = \frac{1}{4n^2} (\sin a + \sin b + \sin c)^2 - 1.$$

We have

$$4n^2 = 1 - \cos^2 a - \cos^2 b - \cos^2 c + 2 \cos a \cos b \cos c;$$

therefore
$$(\sin a + \sin b + \sin c)^2 - 4n^2 = 2(1 + \sin a \sin b + \sin b \sin c$$
$$+ \sin c \sin a - \cos a \cos b \cos c).$$

Also

$$\cot r + \tan R = \frac{1}{2n} \{\sin s + \sin(s-a) + \sin(s-b) + \sin(s-c)\};$$

and by squaring both members of this equation the required result will be obtained. For it may be shewn by reduction that

$$\sin^2 s + \sin^2 (s-a) + \sin^2 (s-b) + \sin^2 (s-c)$$
$$= 2 - 2\cos a \cos b \cos c,$$

and

$$\sin s \sin(s-a) + \sin s \sin(s-b) + \sin s \sin(s-c)$$
$$+ \sin(s-a) \sin(s-b) + \sin(s-b) \sin(s-c) + \sin(s-c)$$
$$\sin(s-a) = \sin a \sin b + \sin b \sin c + \sin c \sin a.$$

Similarly we may prove that

$$(\cot r_1 - \tan R)^2 = \frac{1}{4n^2}(\sin b + \sin c - \sin a)^2 - 1.$$

95. In the figure to Art. 89, suppose DP produced through P to a point A'. such that DA' is a quadrant, then A' is a pole of BC, and $PA' = \dfrac{\pi}{2} - r$; similarly, suppose EP produced through P to a point B. such that EB. is a quadrant, and FP produced through P to a point C' such that FC' is a quadrant. Then $A'B'C'$ is the polar triangle of ABC, and $PA' = PB' = PC' = \dfrac{\pi}{2} - r$. Thus P is the pole of the small circle *described round* the polar triangle, and the angular radius of the small circle *described round* the polar triangle is the complement of the angular radius of the small circle inscribed in the primitive triangle. And in like manner the point which is the pole of the small circle inscribed in the polar triangle is also the pole of

the small circle described round the primitive triangle, and the angular radii of the two circles are complementary.

EXAMPLES

In the following examples the notation of the Chapter is retained. Shew that in any triangle the following relations hold contained in Examples 1 to 7:

1. $\tan r_1 \tan r_2 \tan r_3 = \tan r \sin^2 s$.

2. $\tan R + \cot r = \tan R_1 + \cot r_1 = \tan R_2 + \cot r_2$

$$= \tan R_3 + \cot r_3 = \frac{1}{2}(\cot r + \cot r_1 + \cot r_2 + \cot r_3).$$

3. $\tan^2 R + \tan^2 R_1 + \tan^2 R_2 + \tan^2 R_3$

$$= \cot^2 r + \cot^2 r_1 + \cot^2 r_2 + \cot^2 r_3.$$

4. $\dfrac{\tan r_1 + \tan r_2 + \tan r_3 + \tan r}{\cot r_1 + \cot r_2 + \cot r_3 - \cot r}$

$$= \frac{1}{2}(1 + \cos a + \cos b + \cos c).$$

5. $\operatorname{cosec}^2 r = \cot(s-a)\cot(s-b) + \cot(s-b)\cot(s-c) + \cot(s-c)(s-a).$

6. $\operatorname{cosec}^2 r_1 = \cot(s-b)\cot(s-c) - \cot s \cot(s-b) - \cot s \cot(s-c).$

7. $\tan R_1 \tan R_2 \tan R_3 = \tan R \sec^2 S$.

8. Shew that in an equilateral triangle $\tan R = 2 \tan r$.

9. If ABC be an equilateral spherical triangle, P the pole of the circle circumscribing it, Q any point on the sphere, shew that

$$\cos QA + \cos QB + \cos QC = 3 \cos PA \cos PQ.$$

10. If three small circles be inscribed in a spherical triangle having each of its angles 120°, so that each touches the other two as well as two sides of the triangle, shew that the radius of each of the small circles = 30°, and that the centres of the three small circles coincide with the angular points of the polar triangle.

AREA OF A SPHERICAL TRIANGLE SPHERICAL EXCESS

96. *To find the area of a Lune.*

A *Lune* is that portion of the surface of a sphere which is comprised between two great semicircles.

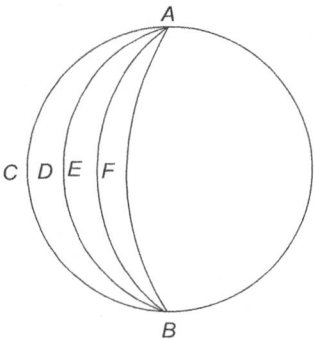

Let *ACBDA*, *ADBEA* be two lunes having equal angles at *A*; then one of these lunes may be supposed placed on the other so as to coincide exactly with it; thus *lunes having equal angles are equal*. Then by a process similar to that used in the first proposition of the Sixth Book of Euclid it may be shewn that *lunes are proportional to their angles*. Hence since the whole surface of a sphere may be considered as a lune with an angle equal to four right angles, we have for a lune with an angle of which the circular measure is A,

$$\frac{\text{area of lune}}{\text{surface of sphere}} = \frac{A}{2\pi}.$$

Suppose r the radius of the sphere, then the surface is $4\pi r^2$ (*Integral Calculus*, Chap. VII.); thus

$$\text{area of lune} = \frac{A}{2\pi} 4\pi r^2 = 2Ar^2.$$

97. *To find the area of a Spherical Triangle.*

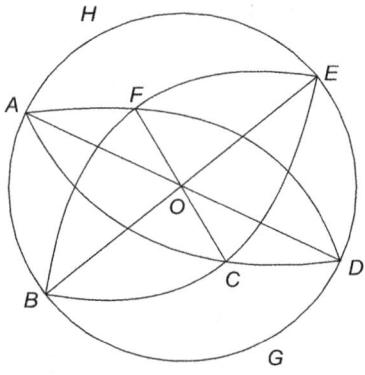

Let ABC be a spherical triangle; produce the arcs which form its sides until they meet again two and two, which will happen when each has become equal to the semicircumference. The triangle ABC now forms a part of three lunes, namely, $ABDCA$, $BCEAB$, and $CAFBC$. Now the triangles CDE

and *AFB* are subtended by vertically opposite solid angles at *O*, and *we will assume* that their areas are equal; therefore the lune *CAFBC* is equal to the sum of the two triangles *ABC* and *CDE*. Hence if *A, B, C* denote the circular measures of the angles of the triangle, we have

triangle $ABC + BGDC$ = lune $ABDCA = 2Ar^2$,

triangle $ABC + AHEC$ = lune $BCEAB = 2Br^2$,

triangle ABC + triangle CDE = lune $CAFBC = 2Cr^2$;

hence, by addition,

twice triangle ABC + surface of hemisphere = $2(A + B + C)r^2$;

therefore   triangle $ABC = (A + B + C - \pi)r^2$.

The expression $A + B + C - \pi$ is called the *spherical excess* of the triangle; and since

$$(A + B + C - \pi)r^2 = \frac{A + B + C - \pi}{2\pi} 2\pi r^2,$$

the result obtained may be thus enunciated: *the area of a spherical triangle is the same fraction of half the surface of the sphere as the spherical excess is of four right angles.*

98. We have assumed, as is usually done, that the areas of the triangles *CDE* and *AFB* in the preceding Article are equal. The triangles are, however, not absolutely equal, but *symmetrically* equal (Art. 57), so that one cannot be made to coincide with the other by superposition. It is, however, easy to decompose two such triangles into pieces which admit

of superposition, and thus to prove that their areas are equal. For describe a small circle round each, then the angular radii of these circles will be equal by Art. 92. If the pole of the circumscribing circle falls inside each triangle, then each triangle is the sum of three isosceles triangles, and if the pole falls outside each triangle, then each triangle is the excess of two isosceles triangles over a third; and in each case the isosceles triangles of one set are respectively *absolutely equal* to the corresponding isosceles triangles of the other set.

99. *To find the area of a spherical polygon.*

Let n be the number of sides of the polygon, Σ the sum of all its angles. Take any point within the polygon and join it with all the angular points; thus the figure is divided into n triangles. Hence, by Art. 97,

area of polygon = (sum of the angles of the triangles $- n\pi)r^2$,

and the sum of the angles of the triangles is equal to Σ together with the four right angles which are formed round the common vertex; therefore

$$\text{area of polygon } = \{\Sigma - (n-2)\pi\}\, r^2.$$

This expression is true even when the polygon has some of its angles greater than two right angles, provided it can be decomposed into triangles, of which each of the angles is less than two right angles.

100. We shall now give some expressions for certain trigonometrical functions of the *spherical excess* of a triangle. We denote the spherical excess by E, so that $E = A + B + C - \pi$.

101. *Cagnoli's Theorem*. To shew that

$$\sin \frac{1}{2} E = \frac{\sqrt{\{\sin s \sin(s-a)\sin(s-b)\sin(s-c)\}} \, x}{2\cos\frac{1}{2}a\cos\frac{1}{2}b\cos\frac{1}{2}c}.$$

$$\sin\frac{1}{2}E = \sin\frac{1}{2}(A+B+C-\pi) = \sin\left\{\frac{1}{2}(A+B) - \frac{1}{2}(\pi-C)\right\}$$

$$= \sin\frac{1}{2}(A+B)\sin\frac{1}{2}C - \cos\frac{1}{2}(A+B)\cos\frac{1}{2}C$$

$$= \frac{\sin\frac{1}{2}C\cos\frac{1}{2}C}{\cos\frac{1}{2}c}\left\{\cos\frac{1}{2}(a-b) - \cos\frac{1}{2}(a-b)\right\},$$
$$\text{(Art.54),}$$

$$= \frac{\sin C \sin\frac{1}{2}a\sin\frac{1}{2}b}{\cos\frac{1}{2}c}$$

$$= \frac{\sin\frac{1}{2}a\sin\frac{1}{2}b}{\cos\frac{1}{2}c} \cdot \frac{2}{\sin a \sin b}.$$

$$= \frac{\sqrt{\{\sin s \sin(s-a)\sin(s-b)\sin(s-c)\}}}{\sqrt{\{\sin s \sin(s-a)\sin(s-b)\sin(s-c)\}}}$$
$$= \frac{\sqrt{\{\sin s \sin(s-a)\sin(s-b)\sin(s-c)\}}}{2\cos\frac{1}{2}a\cos\frac{1}{2}b\cos\frac{1}{2}c}.$$

102. *Lhuilier's Theorem*. To shew that

$$\tan\frac{1}{4}E = \sqrt{\{\tan\frac{1}{2}s\tan\frac{1}{2}(s-a)\tan\frac{1}{2}(s-b)\tan\frac{1}{2}(s-c)\}}.$$

$$\tan \frac{1}{4} E = \frac{\sin \frac{1}{2}(A+B+C-\pi)}{\cos \frac{1}{4}(A+B+C-\pi)}$$

$$= \frac{\sin \frac{1}{2}(A+B) - \sin \frac{1}{2}(\pi - C)}{\cos \frac{1}{2}(A+B) + \cos \frac{1}{2}(\pi - C)}, \quad (\textit{Plane Trig}.\text{Art}.84),$$

$$= \frac{\sin \frac{1}{2}(A+B) - \cos \frac{1}{2}C}{\cos \frac{1}{2}(A+B) + \sin \frac{1}{2}C}$$

$$= \frac{\cos \frac{1}{2}(a-b) - \cos \frac{1}{2}c}{\cos \frac{1}{2}(a+b) + \cos \frac{1}{2}c} \cdot \frac{\cos \frac{1}{2}C}{\sin \frac{1}{2}C}, \quad (\text{Art}.54)$$

Hence, by Art. 45, we obtain

$$\tan \frac{1}{4} E = \frac{\sin \frac{1}{4}(c+a-b)\sin \frac{1}{4}(c+b-a)}{\cos \frac{1}{4}(a+b+c)\cos \frac{1}{4}(a+b-c)}$$

$$\sqrt{\left\{ \frac{\sin s \sin(s-c)}{\sin(s-a)\sin(s-b)} \right\}}$$

$$= \sqrt{\left\{ \tan \frac{1}{2}s \tan \frac{1}{2}(s-a)\tan \frac{1}{2}(s-b)\tan \frac{1}{2}(s-c) \right\}}.$$

103.   We may obtain many other formulae involving trigonometrical functions of the spherical excess. Thus, for example,

$$\cos \frac{1}{2} E = \cos \left\{ \frac{1}{2}(A+B) - \frac{1}{2}(\pi - C) \right\}$$

$$= \cos \frac{1}{2}(A+B)\sin \frac{1}{2}C + \sin \frac{1}{2}(A+B)\cos \frac{1}{2}C$$

$$= \left\{ \cos\frac{1}{2}(a+b)\sin^2\frac{1}{2}C + \cos\frac{1}{2}(a-b)\cos^2\frac{1}{2}C \right\} \sec\frac{1}{2}c,$$

$$\text{(Art.54)},$$

$$= \left\{ \cos\frac{1}{2}a\cos\frac{1}{2}b\left(\cos^2 C + \sin^2\frac{1}{2}C \right) \right.$$

$$\left. + \sin\frac{1}{2}a\sin\frac{1}{2}b\left(\cos^2\frac{1}{2}C - \sin^2\frac{1}{2}C \right) \right\} \sec\frac{1}{2}c$$

$$= \left\{ \cos\frac{1}{2}a\cos\frac{1}{2}b + \sin\frac{1}{2}a\sin\frac{1}{2}b\cos C \right\} \sec\frac{1}{2}c. \qquad (1)$$

Again, it was shewn in Art. 101, that

$$\sin\frac{1}{2}E = \sin C \sin\frac{1}{2}a \sin\frac{1}{2}b \sec\frac{1}{2}c;$$

therefore

$$\tan\frac{1}{2}E = \frac{\sin\frac{1}{2}a\sin\frac{1}{2}b\sin C}{\cos\frac{1}{2}a\cos\frac{1}{2}b + \sin\frac{1}{2}a\sin\frac{1}{2}b\cos C}. \qquad (2)$$

Again, we have from above

$$\cos\frac{1}{2}E = \left\{ \cos\frac{1}{2}a\cos\frac{1}{2}b + \sin\frac{1}{2}a\sin\frac{1}{2}b\cos C \right\} \sec\frac{1}{2}c$$

$$= \frac{(1+\cos a)(1+\cos b) + \sin a \sin b \cos C}{4\cos\frac{1}{2}a\cos\frac{1}{2}b\cos\frac{1}{2}c}$$

$$= \frac{1+\cos a + \cos b \cos c}{4\cos\frac{1}{2}a\cos\frac{1}{2}b\cos\frac{1}{2}c} = \frac{\cos^2\frac{1}{2}a + \cos^2\frac{1}{2}b + \cos^2\frac{1}{2}c - 1}{2\cos\frac{1}{2}a\cos\frac{1}{2}b\cos\frac{1}{2}c}. \cdot(3)$$

In (3) put $1 - 2\sin^2\frac{1}{4}E$ for $\cos\frac{1}{2}E$; thus

$$\sin^2\frac{1}{4}E = \frac{1 + 2\cos\frac{1}{2}a\cos\frac{1}{2}b\cos\frac{1}{2}c - \cos^2\frac{1}{2}a - \cos^2\frac{1}{2}b - \cos^2\frac{1}{2}c}{4\cos\frac{1}{2}a\cos\frac{1}{2}b\cos\frac{1}{2}c}.$$

By ordinary development we can shew that the numerator of the above fraction is equal to

$$4\sin\frac{1}{2}s\sin\frac{1}{2}(s-a)\sin\frac{1}{2}(s-b)\sin\frac{1}{2}(s-c);$$

therefore

$$\sin^2\frac{1}{4}E = \frac{\sin\frac{1}{2}s\sin\frac{1}{2}(s-a)\sin\frac{1}{2}(s-b)\sin\frac{1}{2}(s-c)}{\cos\frac{1}{2}a\cos\frac{1}{2}b\cos\frac{1}{2}c}. \quad (4)$$

Similarly

$$\cos^2\frac{1}{4}E = \frac{\cos\frac{1}{2}s\cos\frac{1}{2}(s-a)\cos\frac{1}{2}(s-b)\cos\frac{1}{2}(s-c)}{\cos\frac{1}{2}a\cos\frac{1}{2}b\cos\frac{1}{2}c}. \quad (5)$$

Hence by division we obtain Lhuilier's Theorem.

Again,

$$\frac{\sin(C - \frac{1}{2}E)}{\sin\frac{1}{2}E} = \sin C \cot\tfrac{1}{2}E - \cos C$$

$$= \sin C \frac{\cos\frac{1}{2}a\cos\frac{1}{2}b + \sin\frac{1}{2}a\sin\frac{1}{2}b\cos C}{\sin\frac{1}{2}a\sin\frac{1}{2}b\sin C}$$

$$- \cos C, \text{ by (2)},$$

$$= \cos\frac{1}{2}a\cot\frac{1}{2}b;$$

therefore, by Art. 101,

$$\sin(C - \frac{1}{2}E) = \frac{\sqrt{\{\sin s \sin(s-a)\sin(s-b)\sin(s-c)\}}}{2\sin\frac{1}{2}a\sin\frac{1}{2}b\cos\frac{1}{2}c}.$$

Again,

$$\cos\left(C - \frac{1}{2}E\right) = \cos C \cos\frac{1}{2}E + \sin C \sin\frac{1}{2}E$$

$$= \frac{(1+\cos a)(1+\cos b)\cos C + \sin a \sin b \cos^2 C}{4\cos\frac{1}{2}a\cos\frac{1}{2}b\cos\frac{1}{2}c}$$

$$+ \sin^2 C \sin\tfrac{1}{2}a\sin\tfrac{1}{2}b\sec\tfrac{1}{2}c$$

$$= \frac{(1+\cos a)(1+\cos b)\cos C + \sin a \sin b}{4\cos\frac{1}{2}a\cos\frac{1}{2}b\cos\frac{1}{2}c}$$

$$= \left\{\cos\frac{1}{2}a\cos\frac{1}{2}b\cos C + \sin\frac{1}{2}a\sin\frac{1}{2}b\right\}\sec\frac{1}{2}c$$

$$= \frac{\sin a \sin b \cos C + 4\sin^2\frac{1}{2}a\sin^2\frac{1}{2}b}{4\sin\frac{1}{2}a\sin\frac{1}{2}b\cos\frac{1}{2}c}$$

$$= \frac{\cos c - \cos a \cos b + (1-\cos a)(1-\cos b)}{4\sin\frac{1}{2}a\sin b\cos\frac{1}{2}c}$$

$$= \frac{1 + \cos c - \cos a - \cos b}{4 \sin \frac{1}{2} a \sin \frac{1}{2} b \cos \frac{1}{2} c}$$

$$= \frac{\cos^2 \frac{1}{2} c - \cos^2 \frac{1}{2} a - \cos^2 \frac{1}{2} b + 1}{2 \sin \frac{1}{2} a \sin \frac{1}{2} b \cos \frac{1}{2} c}. \tag{6}$$

From this result we can deduce two other results, in the same manner as (4) and (5) were deduced from (3); or we may observe that the right-hand member of (6) can be obtained from the right-hand member of (3) by writing $\pi - a$ and $\pi - b$ for a and b respectively, and thus we may deduce the results more easily. We shall have then

$$\sin^2\left(\frac{1}{2}C - \frac{1}{4}E\right) = \frac{\cos\frac{1}{2}s\,\sin\frac{1}{2}(s-a)\sin\frac{1}{2}(s-b)\cos\frac{1}{2}(s-c)}{\sin\frac{1}{2}a\,\sin\frac{1}{2}b\,\cos\frac{1}{2}c},$$

$$\cos^2\left(\frac{1}{2}C - \frac{1}{4}E\right) = \frac{\sin\frac{1}{2}s\,\cos\frac{1}{2}(s-a)\cos\frac{1}{2}(s-b)\sin\frac{1}{2}(s-c)}{\sin\frac{1}{2}a\,\sin\frac{1}{2}b\,\cos\frac{1}{2}c}.$$

EXAMPLES

1. Find the angles and sides of an equilateral triangle whose area is one-fourth of that of the sphere on which it is described.

2. Find the surface of an equilateral and equiangular spherical polygon of n sides, and determine the value of each of the angles when the surface equals half the surface of the sphere.

3. If $a = b = \dfrac{\pi}{3}$, and $c = \dfrac{\pi}{2}$, shew that $E = \cos^{-1}\dfrac{7}{9}$.

4. If the angle C of a spherical triangle be a right angle, shew that

$$\sin\frac{1}{2}E = \sin\frac{1}{2}a\sin\frac{1}{2}b\sec\frac{1}{2}c, \quad \cos\frac{1}{2}E$$

$$= \cos\frac{1}{2}a\cos\frac{1}{2}b\sec\frac{1}{2}c.$$

5. If the angle C be a right angle, shew that

$$\frac{\sin^2 c}{\cos c}\cos E = \frac{\sin^2 a}{\cos a} + \frac{\sin^2 b}{\cos b}.$$

6. If $a=b$ and $C=\dfrac{\pi}{2}$, shew that $\tan E = \dfrac{\sin^2 a}{2\cos a}$.

7. The sum of the angles in a right-angled triangle is less than four right angles.

8. Draw through a given point in the side of a spherical triangle an arc of a great circle cutting off a given part of the triangle.

9. In a spherical triangle if

$$\cos C = 1\tan\frac{a}{2}\tan\frac{b}{2}, \text{ then } C = A + B.$$

10. If the angles of a spherical triangle be together equal to four right angles

$$\cos^2\frac{1}{2}a + \cos^2\frac{1}{2}b + \cos^2\frac{1}{2}c = 1.$$

11. If r^1, r^2, r^3 be the radii of three small circles of a sphere of radius r which touch one another at P, Q, R, and A, B, C be the angles of the spherical triangle formed by joining their centres,

$$\text{area } PQR = (A \cos r_1 + B \cos r_2 + C \cos r_3 - \pi)r^2.$$

12. Shew that

$$\sin s = \frac{\left\{ \sin \frac{1}{2} E \sin(A - \frac{1}{2} E) \sin(B - \frac{1}{2} E) \sin(C - \frac{1}{2} E) \right\}^{\frac{1}{2}}}{2 \sin \frac{1}{2} A \sin \frac{1}{2} B \sin \frac{1}{2} C}.$$

13. Given two sides of a spherical triangle, determine when the area is a maximum.

14. Find the area of a regular polygon of a given number of sides formed by arcs of great circles on the surface of a sphere; and hence deduce that, if α be the angular radius of a small circle, its area is to that of the whole surface of the sphere as versin α is to 2.

15. A, B, C are the angular points of a spherical triangle; A', B', C' are the middle points of the respectively opposite sides. If E be the spherical excess of the triangle, shew that

$$\cos \frac{1}{2} E = \frac{\cos A'B'}{\cos \frac{1}{2} c} = \frac{\cos B'C'}{\cos \frac{1}{2} a} = \frac{\cos C'A'}{\cos \frac{1}{2} b}.$$

16. If one of the arcs of great circles which join the middle points of the sides of a spherical triangle be a quadrant, shew that the other two are also quadrants.

ON CERTAIN APPROXIMATE FORMULAE

104. We shall now investigate certain approximate formulæ which are often useful in calculating spherical triangles when the radius of the sphere is large compared with the lengths of the sides of the triangles.

105. *Given two sides and the included angle of a spherical triangle, to find the angle between the chords of these sides.*

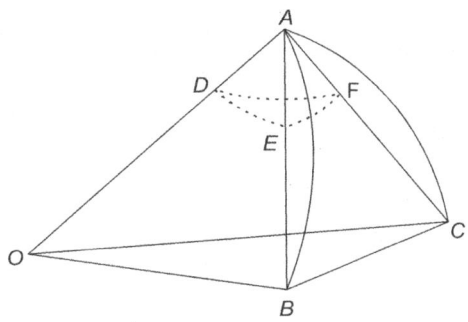

Let AB, AC be the two sides of the triangle ABC; let O be the centre of the sphere. Describe a sphere round A as a centre, and suppose it to meet AO, AB, AC at D, E, F respectively. Then the angle EDF is the inclination of the planes OAB, OAC, and is therefore equal to A. From the spherical triangle DEF

$$\cos EF = \cos DE \cos DF + \sin DE \sin DF \cos A;$$

and $\qquad DE = \frac{1}{2}(\pi - c),\ DF = \frac{1}{2}(\pi - b);$

therefore $\cos EF = \sin\frac{1}{2}b\sin\frac{1}{2}c + \cos\frac{1}{2}b\cos\frac{1}{2}c\cos A.$

If the sides of the triangle are small compared with the radius of the sphere, EF will not differ much from A; suppose $EF = A - \theta$, then approximately

$$\cos EF = \cos A + \theta \sin A;$$

and $\quad \sin\frac{1}{2}b\sin\frac{1}{2}c = \sin^2\frac{1}{4}(b+c) - \sin^2\frac{1}{4}(b-c),$

$$\cos\frac{1}{2}b\cos\frac{1}{2}c = \cos^2\frac{1}{4}(b+c) - \sin^2\frac{1}{4}(b-c);$$

therefore

$$\cos A + \theta \sin A = \sin^2\frac{1}{4}(b+c) - \sin^2\frac{1}{4}(b-c)$$
$$+ \left\{1 - \sin^2\frac{1}{4}(b+c) - \sin^2\frac{1}{4}(b-c)\right\}\cos A;$$

therefore

$$\theta \sin A = (1 - \cos A)\sin^2 \frac{1}{4}(b+c) - (1 + \cos A)\sin^2 \frac{1}{4}(b-c),$$

therefore $\quad \theta = \tan\frac{1}{2}A\sin^2\frac{1}{4}(b+c) - \cot\frac{1}{2}A\sin^2\frac{1}{4}(b-c).$

This gives the *circular measure* of θ; the number of seconds in the angle is found by dividing the circular measure by the circular measure of one second, or approximately by the sine of one second (*Plane Trigonometry*, Art. 123). If the lengths of the arcs corresponding to a and b respectively be α and β, and r the radius of the sphere, we have $\dfrac{\alpha}{r}$ and $\dfrac{\beta}{r}$ as the circular measures of a and b respectively; and the lengths of the sides of the chordal triangle are $2r\sin\dfrac{\alpha}{2r}$ and $2r\sin\dfrac{\beta}{2r}$ respectively. Thus when the sides of the spherical triangle and the radius of the sphere are known, we can calculate the angles and sides of the chordal triangle.

106. *Legendre's Theorem. If the sides of a spherical triangle be small compared with the radius of the sphere, then each angle of the spherical triangle exceeds by one third of the spherical excess the corresponding angle of the plane triangle, the sides of which are of the same length as the arcs of the spherical triangle.*

Let A, B, C be the angles of the spherical triangle; a, b, c the sides; r the radius of the sphere; α, β, γ the lengths of the arcs which form the sides, so that $\dfrac{\alpha}{r}, \dfrac{\beta}{r}, \dfrac{\gamma}{r}$ are the circular measures of a, b, c respectively. Then

now $\qquad \cos A = \dfrac{\cos a - \cos b \cos c}{\sin b \sin c};$

$$\cos a = 1 - \dfrac{\alpha^2}{2r^2} + \dfrac{\alpha^4}{24r^4} - \dots,$$

$$\sin a = \dfrac{\alpha}{r} - \dfrac{\alpha^3}{6r^3} + \dots.$$

Similar expressions hold for $\cos b$ and $\sin b$, and for $\cos c$ and $\sin c$ respectively. Hence, if we neglect powers of the circular measure above the *fourth*, we have

$$\cos A = \dfrac{1 - \dfrac{\alpha^2}{2r^2} + \dfrac{\alpha^4}{24r^4} - \left(1 - \dfrac{\beta^2}{2r^2} + \dfrac{\beta^4}{24r^4}\right)\left(1 - \dfrac{\gamma^2}{2r^2} + \dfrac{\gamma^4}{24r^4}\right)}{\dfrac{\beta\gamma}{r^2}\left(1 - \dfrac{\beta^2}{6r^2}\right)\left(1 - \dfrac{\gamma^2}{6r^2}\right)}$$

$$= \dfrac{\dfrac{1}{2r^2}(\beta^2 + \gamma^2 - \alpha^2) + \dfrac{1}{24r^4}(\alpha^4 - \beta^4 - \gamma^4 - 6\beta^2\gamma^2)}{\dfrac{\beta\gamma}{r^2}\left(1 - \dfrac{\beta^2 + \gamma^2}{6r^2}\right)}$$

$$= \dfrac{1}{2\beta\gamma}\left\{\beta^2 + \gamma^2 - \alpha^2 + \dfrac{1}{12r^2}(\alpha^2 - \beta^2 - \gamma^2 - 6\beta^2\gamma^2)\right\}$$

$$\qquad \left\{1 + \dfrac{\beta^2 + \gamma^2}{6r^2}\right\}$$

$$= \dfrac{\beta^2 + \gamma^2 - \alpha^2}{2\beta\gamma} + \dfrac{\alpha^4 + \beta^4 + \gamma^4 - 2\alpha^2\beta^2 - 2\beta^2\gamma^2 - 2\gamma^2\alpha^2}{24\beta\gamma r^2}.$$

Now let A', B', C' be the angles of the plane triangle whose sides are α, β, γ respectively; then

$$\cos A' = \frac{\beta^2 + \gamma^2 - \alpha^2}{2\beta\gamma},$$

thus

$$\cos A = \cos A' - \frac{\beta\gamma \sin^2 A'}{6r^2}.$$

Suppose $A = A' + \theta$; then

$$\cos A = \cos A' - \theta \sin A' \text{ approximately};$$

therefore

$$\theta = \frac{\beta\gamma \sin A'}{6r^2} = \frac{S}{3r^2},$$

where S denotes the area of the plane triangle whose sides are α, β, γ. Similarly

$$B = B' + \frac{S}{3r^2} \text{ and } C = C' + \frac{S}{3r^2};$$

hence approximately

$$A + B + C = A' + B' + C' + \frac{S}{r^2} = \pi + \frac{S}{r^2};$$

therefore $\dfrac{S}{r^2}$ is approximately equal to the spherical excess of the spherical triangle, and thus the theorem is established.

It will be seen that in the above approximation the area of the spherical triangle is considered equal to the area of the plane triangle which can be formed with sides of the same length.

107. Legendre's Theorem may be used for the approximate solution of spherical triangles in the following manner.

1. Suppose the three sides of a spherical triangle known; then the values of α, β, γ are known, and by the formulæ of Plane Trigonometry we can calculate S and A', B', C'; then A, B, C are known from the formulæ.

$$A = A' + \frac{S}{3r^2}, B = B' + \frac{S}{3r^2}, C = C' + \frac{S}{3r^2}.$$

2. Suppose two sides and the included angle of a spherical triangle known, for example A, b, c. Then

$$S = \frac{1}{2}\beta\gamma\sin A' = \frac{1}{2}\beta\gamma\sin A \text{ approximately.}$$

Then A' is known from the formula $A' = A - \dfrac{S}{3r^2}$. Thus in the plane triangle two sides and the included angle are known; therefore its remaining parts can be calculated, and then those of the spherical triangle become known.

3. Suppose two sides and the angle opposite to one of them in a spherical triangle known, for example A, a, b. Then

$$\sin B' = \frac{\beta}{\alpha}\sin A' = \frac{\beta}{\alpha}\sin A \text{ approximately;}$$

and $C' = \pi - A' - B' = \pi - A - B'$ approximately; then $S = \dfrac{1}{2}\alpha\beta \sin C'$. Hence A' is known and the plane triangle can be solved, since two sides and the angle opposite to one of them are known.

4. Suppose two angles and the included side of a spherical triangle known, for example A, B, c.

Then $S = \dfrac{\gamma^2 \sin A' \sin B'}{2\sin(A' + B')} = \dfrac{\gamma^2 \sin A \sin B}{2\sin(A + B)}$ nearly.

Hence in the plane triangle two angles and the included side are known.

5. Suppose two angles and the side opposite to one of them in a spherical triangle known, for example A, B, a. Then

$C' = \pi - A' - B' = \pi - A - B$, approximately, and

$$S = \dfrac{\alpha^2 \sin B' \sin C'}{2\sin(B' + C')},$$

which can be calculated, since B' and C' are approximately known.

108. The importance of Legendre's Theorem in the application of Spherical Trigonometry to the measurement of the Earth's surface has given rise to various developments of it which enable us to test the degree of exactness of the approximation. We shall finish the present Chapter with some

of these developments, which will serve as exercises for the student. We have seen that approximately the spherical excess is equal to $\dfrac{S}{r^2}$, and we shall begin with investigating a closer approximate formula for the spherical excess.

109. *To find an approximate value of the spherical excess.*

Let E denote the spherical excess; then

$$\sin\frac{1}{2}E = \frac{\sin\frac{1}{2}a\,\sin\frac{1}{2}b\,\sin C}{\cos\frac{1}{2}c};$$

therefore approximately

$$\sin\frac{1}{2}E = \sin C\,\frac{\alpha\beta}{4r^2}\left(1-\frac{\alpha^2}{24r^2}\right)\left(1-\frac{\beta^2}{24r^2}\right)\left(1-\frac{\gamma^2}{8r^2}\right)^{-1}$$

$$= \sin C\,\frac{\alpha\beta}{4r^2}\left(1+\frac{3\gamma^2-\alpha^2-\beta^2}{24r^2}\right);$$

therefore $E = \sin C\,\dfrac{\alpha\beta}{2r^2}\left(1+\dfrac{3\gamma^2-\alpha^2-\beta^2}{24r^2}\right),$ \hfill (1)

and $\sin C = \sin\left(C'+\dfrac{1}{3}E\right) = \sin C' + \dfrac{1}{3}E\cos C'$

$$= \sin C' + \frac{\sin C' \cos C'}{3}\frac{\alpha\beta}{2r^2}$$

$$= \sin C'\left(1+\frac{\alpha^2+\beta^2-\gamma^2}{12r^2}\right).$$ \hfill (2)

From (1) and (2)

$$E = \sin C' \frac{\alpha\beta}{2r^2}\left(1 + \frac{\alpha^2 + \beta^2 + \gamma^2}{24r^2}\right).$$

Hence to this order of approximation the area of the spherical triangle exceeds that of the plane triangle by the fraction $\dfrac{\alpha^2 + \beta^2 + \gamma^2}{24r^2}$ of the latter.

110. *To find an approximate value of* $\dfrac{\sin A}{\sin B}$.

$$\frac{\operatorname{Sin} A}{\operatorname{Sin} B} = \frac{\sin a}{\sin b};$$

hence approximately $\dfrac{\sin A}{\sin B} = \dfrac{\alpha\left(1 - \frac{\alpha^2}{6r^2} + \frac{\alpha^4}{120r^4}\right)}{\beta\left(1 - \frac{\beta^2}{6r^2} + \frac{\beta^4}{120r^4}\right)}$

$$= \frac{\alpha}{\beta}\left(1 - \frac{\alpha^2}{6r^2} + \frac{\alpha^4}{120r^4} + \frac{\beta^2}{6r^2} - \frac{\alpha^2\beta^2}{36r^4} - \frac{\beta^4}{120r^4} + \frac{\beta^4}{36r^4}\right)$$

$$= \frac{\alpha}{\beta}\left\{1 + \frac{\beta^2 - \alpha^2}{6r^2} + \frac{\alpha^4 - \beta^4}{120r^4} + \frac{\beta^2(\beta^2 - \alpha^2)}{36r^4}\right\}$$

$$= \frac{\alpha}{\beta}\left\{1 + \frac{\beta^2 - \alpha^2}{6r^2}\left(1 + \frac{\beta^2}{6r^2} - \frac{\alpha^2 - \beta^2}{20r^2}\right)\right\}$$

$$= \frac{\alpha}{\beta}\left\{1 + \frac{\beta^2 - \alpha^2}{6r^2}\left(1 + \frac{7\beta^2 - 3\alpha^2}{60r^2}\right)\right\}.$$

111. *To express cot B – cot A approximately.*

$$\cot B - \cot A = \frac{1}{\sin B}\left(\cos B - \frac{\sin B}{\sin A}\cos A\right);$$

hence, approximately, by Art. 110,

$$\cot B - \cot A = \frac{1}{\sin B}\left(\cos B - \frac{\beta}{\alpha}\cos A - \frac{\beta}{\alpha}\frac{\alpha^2 - \beta^2}{6r^2}\cos A\right).$$

Now we have shewn in Art. 106, that approximately

$$\cos A = \frac{\beta^2 + \gamma^2 - \alpha^2}{2\beta\gamma} + \frac{\alpha^4 + \beta^4 + \gamma^4 - 2\alpha^2\beta^2 - 2\beta^2\gamma^2 - 2\gamma^2\alpha^2}{24\beta\gamma r^2},$$

therefore $\cos B - \dfrac{\beta}{\alpha}\cos A = \dfrac{\alpha^2 - \beta^2}{\alpha\gamma}$ approximately,

and $\cot B - \cot A = \dfrac{\alpha^2 - \beta^2}{\alpha\gamma \sin B} - \dfrac{\alpha^2 - \beta^2}{\alpha\gamma \sin B}\dfrac{\beta^2 + \gamma^2 - \alpha^2}{12r^2}$

$$= \frac{\alpha^2 - \beta^2}{\alpha\gamma \sin B}\left(1 - \frac{\beta^2 + \gamma^2 - \alpha^2}{12r^2}\right).$$

112. The approximations in Arts. 109 and 110 are true so far as terms involving r^4; that in Art. 111 is true so far as terms involving r^2, and it will be seen that we are thus able to carry the approximations in the following Article so far as terms involving r^4.

113. *To find an approximate value of the error in the length of a side of a spherical triangle when calculated by Legendre's Theorem.*

Suppose the side β known and the side α required; let 3μ denote the spherical excess which is adopted. Then the approximate value $\dfrac{\beta \sin(A-\mu)}{\sin(B-\mu)}$ is taken for the side of which α is the real value. Let $x = \alpha - \dfrac{\beta(A-\mu)}{\sin(B-\mu)}$; we have then to find x approximately. Now approximately

$$\frac{\sin(A-\mu)}{\sin(B-\mu)} = \frac{\sin A - \mu \cos A - \frac{\mu^2}{2}\sin A}{\sin B - \mu \cos B - \frac{\mu^2}{2}\sin B}$$

$$= \frac{\sin A}{\sin B}\left(1 - \mu \cot A - \frac{\mu^2}{2}\right)\left(1 - \mu \cot B - \frac{\mu^2}{2}\right)^{-1}$$

$$= \frac{\sin A}{\sin B}\{1 + \mu(\cot B - \cot A) + \mu^2 \cot B(\cot B - \cot A)\}$$

$$= \frac{\sin A}{\sin B} + \frac{\mu \sin A}{\sin B}(\cot B - \cot A)(1 + \mu \cot B).$$

Also the following formulæ are true so far as terms involving r^2:

$$\frac{\sin A}{\sin B} = \frac{\alpha}{\beta}\left(1 + \frac{\beta^2 - \alpha^2}{6r^2}\right),$$

$$\cot B - \cot A = \frac{\alpha^2 - \beta^2}{\alpha\gamma \sin B}\left(1 - \frac{\beta^2 + \gamma^2 - \alpha^2}{12r^2}\right),$$

$$1 + \mu \cot B = 1 + \frac{\alpha^2 + \gamma^2 - \beta^2}{12r^2}.$$

Hence, approximately,

$$\frac{\sin A}{\sin B}(\cot B - \cot A)(1 + \mu \cot B) = \frac{\alpha^2 - \beta^2}{\beta \gamma \sin B}.$$

Therefore $\quad x = \alpha - \dfrac{\beta \sin A}{\sin B} - \dfrac{\mu(\alpha^2 - \beta^2)}{\gamma \sin B}$

$$= \frac{\alpha(\beta^2 - \alpha^2)}{6} \left\{ \frac{6\mu}{\alpha \gamma \sin B} - \frac{1}{r^2} + \frac{3\alpha^2 - 7\beta^2}{60r^4} \right\}, \text{ by Art. 110.}$$

If we calculate μ from the formula $\mu = \dfrac{\alpha \gamma \sin B}{6r^2}$ we obtain

$$x = \frac{\alpha(\beta^2 - \alpha^2)(3\alpha^2 - 7\beta^2)}{360r^4}.$$

If we calculate μ from an equation corresponding to (1) of Art. 109, we have

$$\mu = \frac{\alpha \gamma \sin B}{6r^2} \left(1 + \frac{3\beta^2 - \alpha^2 - \gamma^2}{24r^2} \right);$$

therefore $\quad x = \dfrac{\alpha(\beta^2 - \alpha^2)(\alpha^2 + \beta^2 - 5\gamma^2)}{720r^4}.$

MISCELLANEOUS EXAMPLES

1. If the sides of a spherical triangle AB, AC be produced to B', C', so that BB', CC' are the semi-supplements of AB, AC respectively, shew that the arc $B'C'$ will subtend an angle at the centre of the sphere equal to the angle between the chords of AB and AC.

2. Deduce Legendre's Theorem from the formula

$$\tan^2 \frac{A}{2} = \frac{\sin\frac{1}{2}(a+b-c)\sin\frac{1}{2}(c+a-b)}{\sin\frac{1}{2}(b+c-a)\sin\frac{1}{2}(a+b+c)}.$$

3. Four points A, B, C, D on the surface of a sphere are joined by arcs of great circles, and E, F are the middle points of the arcs AC, BD: shew that

$$\cos AB + \cos BC + \cos CD + \cos DA = 4 \cos AE \cos BF \cos FE.$$

4. If a quadrilateral $ABCD$ be inscribed in a small circle on a sphere so that two opposite angles A and C may be at opposite extremities of a diameter, the sum of the cosines of the sides is constant.

5. In a spherical triangle if $A = B = 2C$, shew that

$$\cos a \cos \frac{a}{2} = \cos\left(c + \frac{a}{2}\right).$$

6. *ABC* is a spherical triangle each of whose sides is a quadrant; *P* is any point within the triangle: shew that

$$\cos PA \cos PB \cos PC + \cot BPC \cot CPA \cot APB = 0,$$

and $\tan ABP \tan BCP \tan CAP = 1$.

7. If *O* be the middle point of an equilateral triangle *ABC*, and *P* any point on the surface of the sphere, then

$$\frac{1}{4}(\tan PO \tan OA)^2 (\cos PA + \cos PB + \cos PC)^2$$

$$= \cos^2 PA + \cos^2 PB + \cos^2 PC - \cos PA \cos PB - \cos PB \cos PC - \cos PC \cos PA.$$

8. If *ABC* be a triangle having each side a quadrant, *O* the pole of the inscribed circle, *P* any point on the sphere, then

$$(\cos PA + \cos PB + \cos PC)^2 = 3\cos^2 PO.$$

9. From each of three points on the surface of a sphere arcs are drawn on the surface to three other points situated on a great circle of the sphere, and their cosines are *a*, *b*, *c*; *a'*, *b'*, *c'*; *a''*, *b''*, *c''*. Shew that $ab''c' + a'bc'' + a''b'c = ab'c'' + a'b''c + a''bc'$.

10. From Arts. 110 and 111, shew that approximately

$$\log \beta = \log \alpha + \log \sin B - \log \sin A + \frac{S}{3r^2}(\cot A - \cot B).$$

11. By continuing the approximation in Art. 106 so as to include the terms involving r^4, shew that approximately

$$\cos A = \cos A' - \frac{\beta\gamma \sin^2 A'}{6r^2} + \frac{\beta\gamma(\alpha^2 - 3\beta^2 - 3\gamma^2)\sin^2 A'}{180r^4}.$$

12. From the preceding result shew that if $A = A' + \theta$ then approximately

$$\theta = \frac{\beta\gamma \sin A'}{6r^2}\left(1 + \frac{7\beta^2 + 7\gamma^2 + \alpha^2}{120r^2}\right).$$

GEODETICAL OPERATIONS

114. One of the most important applications of Trigonometry, both Plane and Spherical, is to the determination of the figure and dimensions of the Earth itself, and of any portion of its surface. We shall give a brief outline of the subject, and for further information refer to Woodhouse's *Trigonometry*, to the article *Geodesy* in the *English Cyclopædia*, and to Airy's treatise on the *Figure of the Earth in the Encyclopædia Metropolitana*. For practical knowledge of the details of the operations it will be necessary to study some of the published accounts of the great surveys which have been effected in different parts of the world, as for example, the *Account of the measurement of two sections of the Meridional arc of India*, by Lieut.-Colonel Everest, 1847; or the *Account of the Observations and Calculations of the Principal Triangulation in the Ordnance Survey of Great Britain and Ireland*, 1858.

115. An important part of any survey consists in the measurement of a horizontal line, which is called a *base*. A level plain of a few miles in length is selected and a line is measured on it with every precaution to ensure accuracy. Rods of deal, and of metal, hollow tubes of glass, and steel chains, have been used in different surveys; the temperature is carefully observed during the operations, and allowance is made for the varying lengths of the rods or chains, which arise from variations in the temperature.

116. At various points of the country suitable stations are selected and signals erected; then by supposing lines to be drawn connecting the signals, the country is divided into a series of triangles. The angles of these triangles are observed, that is, the angles which any two signals subtend at a third. For example, suppose A and B to denote the extremities of the *base*, and C a signal at a third point visible from A and B; then in the triangle ABC the angles ABC and BAC are observed, and then AC and BC can be calculated. Again, let D be a signal at a fourth point, such that it is visible from C and A; then the angles ACD and CAD are observed, and as AC is known, CD and AD can be calculated.

117. Besides the original base other lines are measured in convenient parts of the country surveyed, and their measured lengths are compared with their lengths obtained by calculation through a series of triangles from the original base. The degree of closeness with which the measured length agrees with the calculated length is a test of the accuracy of the survey. During the progress of the Ordnance Survey of Great Britain and Ireland, several lines have been measured;

the last two are, one near Lough Foyle in Ireland, which was measured in 1827 and 1828, and one on Salisbury Plain, which was measured in 1849. The line near Lough Foyle is nearly 8 miles long, and the line on Salisbury Plain is nearly 7 miles long; and the difference between the length of the line on Salisbury Plain as measured and as calculated from the Lough Foyle base is less than 5 inches (*An Account of the Observations* . . . page 419).

118. There are different methods of effecting the calculations for determining the lengths of the sides of all the triangles in the survey. One method is to use the exact formulæ of Spherical Trigonometry. The radius of the Earth may be considered known very approximately; let this radius be denoted by r, then if α be the length of any arc the circular measure of the angle which the arc subtends " at the centre of the earth is $\dfrac{\alpha}{r}$. The formulæ of Spherical Trigonometry gives expressions for the trigonometrical functions of $\dfrac{\alpha}{r}$, so that $\dfrac{\alpha}{r}$ may be found and then α. Since in practice $\dfrac{\alpha}{r}$ is always very small, it becomes necessary to pay attention to the methods of securing accuracy in calculations which involve the logarithmic trigonometrical functions of small angles (*Plane Trigonometry*, Art. 205).

Instead of the exact calculation of the triangles by Spherical Trigonometry, various methods of approximation have been proposed; only two of these methods however have been much used. One method of approximation consists in deducing from the angles of the spherical triangles the angles of the *chordal triangles,* and then computing the latter triangles by Plane Trigonometry (see Art. 105). The other method of approximation consists in the use of Legendre's Theorem (see Art. 106).

119. The three methods which we have indicated were all used by Delambre in calculating the triangles in the French survey (*Base du Systeme Metrique,* Tome III. page 7). In the earlier operations of the Trigonometrical survey of Great Britain and Ireland, the triangles were calculated by the chord method; but this has been for many years discontinued, and in place of it Legendre's Theorem has been universally adopted (*An Account of the Observations* . . . page 244). The triangles in the Indian Survey are stated by Lieut.-Colonel Everest to be computed on Legendre's Theorem. (*An Account of the Measurement* ... page CLVIII.)

120. If the three angles of a plane triangle be observed, the fact that their sum ought to be equal to two right angles affords a test of the accuracy with which the observations are made. We shall proceed to shew how a test of the accuracy of observations of the angles of a spherical triangle formed on the Earth's surface may be obtained by means of the *spherical excess.*

121. *The area of a spherical triangle formed on the Earth's surface being known in square feet, it is required to establish a rule for computing the spherical excess in seconds.*

Let n be the number of seconds in the spherical excess, s the number of square feet in the area of the triangle, r the number of feet in the radius of the Earth. Then if E be the circular measure of the spherical excess,

$$s = Er^2$$

and $\qquad E = \dfrac{n\pi}{160.60.60} = \dfrac{n}{206265}$ approximately;

therefore $\qquad s = \dfrac{nr^2}{206265}.$

Now by actual measurement the mean length of a degree on the Earth's surface is found to be 365155 feet; thus

$$\frac{\pi r}{180} = 365155.$$

With the value of r obtained from this equation it is found by logarithmic calculation, that

$$\log n = \log s - 9.326774.$$

Hence n is known when s is known.

This formula is called General Roy's rule, as it was used by him in the Trigonometrical survey of Great Britain and Ireland. Mr Davies, however, claims it for Mr Dalby. (See Hutton's *Course of Mathematics*, by Davies, Vol. II. p. 47.)

122. In order to apply General Roy's rule, we must know the area of the spherical triangle. Now the area is not known *exactly* unless the elements of the spherical triangle are

known *exactly*; but it is found that in such cases as occur in practice an approximate value of the area is sufficient. Suppose, for example, that we use the area of the *plane triangle* considered in Legendre's Theorem, instead of the area of the *Spherical Triangle itself*; then it appears from Art. 109, that the error is approximately denoted by the fraction $\dfrac{\alpha^2 + \beta^2 + \gamma^2}{24\,r^2}$ of the former area, and this fraction is less than .0001, if the sides do not exceed 100 miles in length. Or again, suppose we want to estimate the influence of errors in the angles on the calculation of the area; let the circular measure of an error be *h*, so that instead of $\dfrac{\alpha\beta \sin C}{2}$ we ought to use $\dfrac{\alpha\beta \sin(C + h)}{2}$; the error then bears to the area approximately the ratio expressed by $h \cot C$. Now in modern observations *h* will not exceed the circular measure of a few seconds, so that, if *C* be not very small, $h \cot C$ is practically insensible.

123. The following example was selected by Woodhouse from the triangles of the English survey, and has been adopted by other writers. The observed angles of a triangle being respectively $42°\,2'32''$, $67°55'39''$, $70°1'48''$, the sum of the errors made in the observations is required, supposing the side opposite to the angle *A* to be 274042 feet. The area is calculated from the expression $\dfrac{a^2 \sin B \sin C}{2 \sin A}$, and by General Roy's rule it is found that $n = .23$. Now the sum of the observed angles is $180° - 1''$, and as it ought to have been $180° + .23''$, it follows that the sum of the errors of the

observations is $1''.23$. This total error may be distributed among the observed angles in such proportion as the opinion of the observer may suggest; one way is to increase each of the observed angles by one-third of $1''.23$, and take the angles thus corrected for the true angles.

124. An investigation has been made with respect to the form of a triangle, in which errors in the observations of the angles will exercise the least influence on the lengths of the sides, and although the reasoning is allowed to be vague it may be deserving of the attention of the student. Suppose the three angles of a triangle observed, and one side, as a, known, it is required to find the form of the triangle in order that the other sides may be least affected by errors in the observations. The spherical excess of the triangle may be supposed known with sufficient accuracy for practice, and if the sum of the observed angles does not exceed two right angles by the proper spherical excess, let these angles be altered by adding the same quantity to each, so as to make their sum correct. Let A, B, C be the angles thus furnished by observation and altered if necessary; and let δA, δB and δC denote the respective errors of A, B and C. Then $\delta A + \delta B + \delta C = 0$, because by supposition the sum of A, B and C is correct.

Considering the triangle as approximately plane, the true value of the side c is

$$\frac{a\sin(C+\delta C)}{\sin(A+\delta A)}, that is, \frac{a\sin(C+\delta C)}{\sin(A-\delta B-\delta C)}.$$

Now approximately

$$\sin(C + \delta C) = \sin C + \delta C \cos C, \text{ (Plane Trigonometry}$$
Chapter 12),

$$\sin(A - \delta B - \delta C) = \sin A - (\delta B + \delta C) \cos A.$$

Hence approximately

$$c = \frac{a \sin C}{\sin A} \{1 + \delta C \cot C\} \{1 - (\delta B + \delta C) \cot A\}^{-1}$$

$$= \frac{a \sin C}{\sin A} \{1 + \delta B \cot A + \delta C (\cot C + \cot A)\};$$

and $\cot C + \cot A = \dfrac{\sin(A+C)}{\sin A \sin C} = \dfrac{\sin B}{\sin A \sin C}$ approximately.

Hence the error of c is approximately

$$\frac{a \sin B}{\sin^2 A} \delta C + \frac{a \sin C \cos A}{\sin A} \delta B.$$

Similarly the error of b is approximately

$$\frac{a \sin C}{\sin^2 A} \delta B + \frac{a \sin B \cos A}{\sin^2 A} \delta C.$$

Now it is impossible to assign exactly the signs and magnitudes of the errors δB and δC, so that the reasoning must be vague. It is obvious that to make the error small $\sin A$ must not be small. And as the sum of δA, δB and δC is zero, two of them must have the same sign, and the third the opposite sign; we may therefore consider that it is more probable than any two as δB and δC have different signs, than that they have the same sign.

If δB and δC have different signs the errors of b and c will be less when cos A is positive than when cos A is negative; A therefore ought to be less than a right angle. And if δB and δC are probably not very different, B and C should be nearly equal. These conditions will be satisfied by a triangle differing not much from an equilateral triangle.

If two angles only, A and B, be observed, we obtain the same expressions as before for the errors in b and c; but we have no reason for considering that δB and δC are of different signs rather than of the same sign. In this case then the supposition that A is a right angle will probably make the errors smallest.

125. The preceding article is taken from the Treatise on Trigonometry in the *Encyclopœdia Metropolitana*. The least satisfactory part is that in which it is considered that δB and δC may be supposed nearly equal; for since $\delta A + \delta B + \delta C = 0$, if we suppose δB and δC nearly equal and of opposite signs, we do in effect suppose $\delta A = 0$ nearly; thus in observing three angles, we suppose that in one observation a certain error is made, in a second observation the same numerical error is made but with an opposite sign, and in the remaining observation no error is made.

126. We have hitherto proceeded on the supposition that the Earth is a sphere; it is however approximately a spheroid of small eccentricity. For the small corrections which must in consequence be introduced into the calculations we must refer to the works named in Art. 114. One of the results obtained is that the error caused by regarding the Earth as a

sphere instead of a spheroid increases with the departure of the triangle from the well-conditioned or equilateral form (*An Account of the Observations* . . . page 243). Under certain circumstances the spherical excess is the same on a spheroid as on a sphere (*Figure of the Earth in the Encyclopædia Metropolitana*, pages 198 and 215).

127. In geodetical operations it is sometimes required to determine the horizontal angle between two points, which are at a small angular distance from the horizon, the angle which the objects subtend being known, and also the angles of elevation or depression.

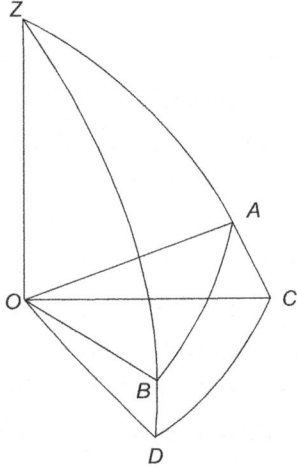

Suppose *OA* and *OB* the directions in which the two points are seen from *O*; and let the angle *AOB* be observed. Let *OZ* be the direction at right angles to the observer's horizon; describe a sphere round *O* as a centre, and let vertical planes through *OA* and *OB* meet the horizon at *OC* and *OD* respectively: then the angle *COD* is required.

Let $AOB = \theta$, $COD = \theta + x$, $AOC = h$, $BOD = k$; from the triangle AZB

$$\cos AZB = \frac{\cos \theta - \cos ZA \cos ZB}{\sin ZA \sin ZB} = \frac{\cos \theta - \sin h \sin k}{\cos h \cos k};$$

and $\cos AZB = \cos COD = \cos(\theta + x)$; thus

$$\cos(\theta + x) = \frac{\cos \theta - \sin h \sin k}{\cos h \cos k}.$$

This formula is exact; by approximation we obtain

$$\cos \theta - x \sin \theta = \frac{\cos \theta - hk}{1 - \frac{1}{2}(h^2 + k^2)};$$

therefore $\quad x \sin \theta = hk - \dfrac{1}{2}(h^2 + k^2) \cos \theta$, nearly,

and $\quad x = \dfrac{2hk - (h^2 + k^2)(\cos^2 \frac{1}{2}\theta - \sin^2 \frac{1}{2}\theta)}{2 \sin \theta}$

$$= \frac{1}{4}(h+k)^2 \tan \frac{1}{2}\theta - \frac{1}{4}(h-k)^2 \cot \frac{1}{2}\theta.$$

This process, by which we find the angle COD from the angle AOB, is called *reducing an angle to the horizon*.

11

ON SMALL VARIATIONS
IN THE PARTS OF A
SPHERICAL TRIANGLE

128. It is sometimes important to know what amount of error will
be introduced into one of the calculated parts of a triangle
by reason of any small error which may exist in the given
parts. We will here consider an example.

129. *A side and the opposite angle of a spherical triangle
remain constant: determine the connexion between the
small variations of any other pair of elements.*

Suppose C and c to remain constant.

1. Required the connexion between the small variations of
    the other sides. We suppose a and b to denote the sides
    of one triangle which can be formed with C and c as
    fixed elements, and $a + \delta a$ and $b + \delta b$ to denote the
    sides of another such triangle; then we require the ratio
    of δa to δb when both are extremely small. We have

    $$\cos c = \cos a \cos b + \sin a \sin b \cos C,$$

and

$$\cos c = \cos(a + \delta a)\cos(b + \delta b) + \sin(a + \delta a)\sin(b + \delta b)\cos C;$$

also $\cos(a + \delta a) = \cos a - \sin a\delta a$, nearly,

and $\sin(a + \delta a) = \sin a + \cos a\delta a$, nearly,

with similar formulæ for $\cos(b + \delta b)$ and $\sin(b + \delta b)$. (See *Plane Trigonometry*, Chapter 12.) Thus

$$\cos c = (\cos a - \sin a\delta a)(\cos b - \sin b\delta b) + (\sin a + \cos a\,\delta a)(\sin b + \cos b\delta b)\cos C.$$

Hence by subtraction, if we neglect the product δa, δb,

$$0 = \delta a(\sin a \cos b - \cos a \sin b \cos C)$$
$$+ \delta b(\sin b \cos a - \cos b \sin a \cos C);$$

this gives the ratio of δa to δb in terms of a, b, C. We may express the ratio more simply in terms of A and B; for, dividing by $\sin a \sin b$, we get from Art. 44,

$$\frac{\delta a}{\sin a}\cot B \sin C + \frac{\delta b}{\sin b}\cot A \sin C = 0;$$

therefore $\delta a \cos B + \delta b \cos A = 0.$

2. Required the connexion between the small variations of the other angles. In this case we may by means of the polar triangle deduce from the result just found, that

$$\delta A \cos b + \delta B \cos a = 0;$$

this may also be found independently as before.

3. Required the connexion between the small variations of a side and the opposite angle (A, a).

Here $\qquad \sin A \sin c = \sin C \sin a,$

and $\quad \sin(A + \delta A) \sin c = \sin C \sin(a + \delta a);$

hence by subtraction

$$\cos A \sin c \delta A = \sin C \cos a \delta a,$$

and therefore $\quad \delta A \cot A = \delta a \cot a.$

4. Required the connexion between the small variations of a side and the adjacent angle (a, B).

We have $\cot C \sin B = \cot c \sin a - \cos B \cos a;$

proceeding as before we obtain

$\cot C \cos B \delta B = \cot c \cos a \delta a + \cos B \sin a \delta a + \cos a \sin B \delta B;$

therefore

$(\cot C \cos B - \cos a \sin B)\, \delta B = (\cot c \cos a + \cos B \sin a)\delta a;$

therefore $\qquad -\dfrac{\cos A}{\sin C} \delta B = \dfrac{\cos b}{\sin c} \delta a;$

therefore $\quad \delta B \cos A = -\delta a \cot b \sin B.$

130. Some more examples are proposed for solution at the end of this Chapter; as they involve no difficulty they are left for the exercise of the student.

EXAMPLES

1.   In a spherical triangle, if C and c remain constant while a and b receive the small increments δa and δb respectively, shew that

$$\frac{\delta a}{\sqrt{(1-n^2\sin^2 a)}} + \frac{\delta b}{\sqrt{(1-n^2\sin^2 b)}} = 0 \quad \text{where } n = \frac{\sin C}{\sin c}.$$

2.   If C and c remain constant, and a small change be made in a, find the consequent changes in the other parts of the triangle. Find also the change in the area.

3.   Supposing A and c to remain constant, prove the following equations, connecting the small variations of pairs of the other elements:

$\sin C\delta b = \sin a\delta B;\ \delta b \sin C = -\delta C \tan a,\ \delta a \tan C = \delta B \sin a,$
$\delta a \tan C = -\delta C \tan a,\ \delta b \cos C = \delta a,\ \delta B \cos a = -\delta C.$

4.   Supposing b and c to remain constant, prove the following equations connecting the small variations of pairs of the other elements:

$\delta B \tan C = \delta C \tan B,\ \delta a \cot C = -\delta B \sin a,\ \delta a = \delta A \sin c \sin B,\ \delta A \sin B \cos C = -\delta B \sin A.$

5.   Supposing B and C to remain constant, prove the following equations connecting the small variations of pairs of the other elements:

$$\delta b \tan c = \delta c \tan b,\ \delta A \cot c = \delta b \sin A,$$

$$\delta A = \delta a \sin b \sin C, \quad \delta a \sin \delta B \cos c = \delta b \sin A.$$

6. If A and C are constant, and b be increased by a small quantity, shew that a will be increased or diminished according as c is less or greater than a quadrant.

ON THE CONNEXION OF FORMULAE IN PLANE AND SPHERICAL TRIGONOMETRY

131. The student must have perceived that many of the results obtained in *Spherical* Trigonometry resemble others with which he is familiar in *Plane* Trigonometry. We shall now pay some attention to this resemblance. We shall first shew how we may deduce formulæ in Plane Trigonometry from formulæ in Spherical Trigonometry; and we shall then investigate some theorems in Spherical Trigonometry which are interesting principally on account of their connexion with known results in Plane Geometry and Trigonometry.

132. *From any formula in Spherical Trigonometry involving the elements of a triangle, one of them being a side, it is required to deduce the corresponding formula in Plane Trigonometry.*

Let α, β, γ be the lengths of the sides of the triangle, r the radius of the sphere, so that $\dfrac{\alpha}{r}, \dfrac{\beta}{r}, \dfrac{\gamma}{r}$ are the circular measures of the sides of the triangle; expand the functions of $\dfrac{\alpha}{r}, \dfrac{\beta}{r}, \dfrac{\gamma}{r}$ which occur in any proposed formula in powers of $\dfrac{\alpha}{r}, \dfrac{\beta}{r}, \dfrac{\gamma}{r}$ respectively; then if we suppose r to become indefinitely great, the limiting form of the proposed formula will be a relation in Plane Trigonometry.

For example, in Art. 106, from the formula

$$\cos A = \frac{\cos a - \cos b \cos c}{\sin b \sin c}$$

we deduce

$$\cos A = \frac{\beta^2 + \gamma^2 - \alpha^2}{2\beta\gamma} + \frac{\alpha^4 + \beta^4 + \gamma^4 - 2\alpha^2\beta^2 - 2\beta^2\gamma^2 - 2\gamma^2\alpha^2}{24\beta\gamma r^2} + \ldots;$$

now suppose r to become infinite; then ultimately

$$\cos A = \frac{\beta^2 + \gamma^2 - \alpha^2}{2\beta\gamma};$$

and this is the expression for the cosine of the angle of a plane triangle in terms of the sides.

Again, in Art. 110, from the formula

$$\frac{\sin A}{\sin B} = \frac{\sin a}{\sin b}$$

we deduce $$\frac{\sin A}{\sin B} = \frac{\alpha}{\beta} + \frac{\alpha(\beta^2 - \alpha^2)}{6\beta r^2} + ...;$$

now suppose r to become infinite; then ultimately

$$\frac{\sin A}{\sin B} = \frac{\alpha}{\beta},$$

that is, in a plane triangle the sides are as the sines of the opposite angles.

133. *To find the equation to a small circle of the sphere.*

The student can easily draw the required diagram.

Let O be the pole of a small circle, S a fixed point on the sphere, SX a fixed great circle of the sphere. Let $OS = \alpha$, $OSX = \beta$; then the position of O is determined by means of these angular co-ordinates α and β. Let P be any point on the circumference of the small circle, $PS = \theta$, $PSX = \phi$, so that θ and ϕ are the angular co-ordinates of P. Let $OP = r$. Then from the triangle OSP

$$\cos r = \cos \alpha \cos \theta + \sin \alpha \sin \theta \cos(\phi - \beta); \qquad (1)$$

this gives a relation between the angular co-ordinates of any point on the circumference of the circle.

If the circle be a great circle then $r = \dfrac{\pi}{2}$; thus the equation becomes

$$0 = \cos\alpha\cos\theta + \sin\alpha\sin\theta\cos(\phi - \beta). \qquad (2)$$

It will be observed that the angular co-ordinates here used are analogous to the *latitude* and *longitude* which serve to determine the positions of places on the Earth's surface; θ is the *complement of the latitude* and ϕ is the *longitude*.

134. Equation (1) of the preceding Article may be written thus:

$$\cos r\left(\cos^2\frac{\theta}{2} + \sin^2\frac{\theta}{2}\right) = \cos\alpha\left(\cos^2\frac{\theta}{2} - \sin^2\frac{\theta}{2}\right)$$
$$+ 2\sin\alpha\sin\frac{\theta}{2}\cos\frac{\theta}{2}\cos(\phi - \beta).$$

Divide by and $\cos^2\dfrac{\theta}{2}$ rearrange; hence

$$\tan^2\frac{\theta}{2}(\cos r + \cos\alpha) - 2\tan\frac{\theta}{2}\sin\alpha\cos(\phi - \beta)$$
$$+ \cos r - \cos\alpha = 0.$$

Let $\tan\dfrac{\theta_1}{2}$ and $\tan\dfrac{\theta_2}{2}$ denote the values of $\tan\dfrac{\theta}{2}$ found from this quadratic equation; then by *Algebra*, Chapter XXII.

$$\tan\frac{\theta_1}{2}\tan\frac{\theta_2}{2} = \frac{\cos r - \cos\alpha}{\cos r + \cos\alpha} = \tan\frac{\alpha + r}{2}\tan\frac{\alpha - r}{2}.$$

Thus the value of the product $\tan \dfrac{\theta_1}{2} \tan \dfrac{\theta_2}{2}$ is *independent of* ϕ; this result corresponds to the well-known property of a circle in Plane Geometry which is demonstrated in Euclid III. 36 *Corollary*.

135. Let three arcs OA, OB, OC meet at a point. From any point P in OB draw PM perpendicular to OA, and PN perpendicular to OC. The student can easily draw the required diagram.

Then, by Art. 65,

$$\sin PM = \sin OP \sin AOB, \quad \sin PN = \sin OP \sin COB;$$

therefore $\qquad \dfrac{\sin PM}{\sin PN} = \dfrac{\sin AOB}{\sin COB}.$

Thus the ratio of $\sin PM$ to $\sin PN$ is independent of the position of P on the arc OB.

136. Conversely suppose that from any other point p arcs pm and pn are drawn perpendicular to OA and OC respectively; then if

$$\dfrac{\sin pm}{\sin pn} = \dfrac{\sin PM}{\sin PN},$$

it will follow that p is on the same great circle as O and P.

137. From two points P_1 and P_2 arcs are drawn perpendicular to a fixed arc; and from a point P on the same great circle as P_1 and P_2 a perpendicular is drawn to the same fixed arc.

Let $PP_1 = \theta_1$ and $PP_2 = \theta_2$; and let the perpendiculars drawn from P, P_1, and P_2 be denoted by x, x_1 and x_2. Then will

$$\sin x = \frac{\sin \theta_2}{\sin(\theta_1 + \theta_2)}\sin x_1 + \frac{\sin \theta_1}{\sin(\theta_1 + \theta_2)}\sin x_2.$$

Let the arc P_1P_2, produced if necessary, cut the fixed arc at a point O; let α denote the angle between the arcs. We will suppose that P_1 is between O and P_2, and that P is between P_1 and P_2.

Then, by Art. 65,

$$\sin x_1 = \sin \alpha \sin OP_1 = \sin \alpha \sin(OP - \theta_1)$$
$$= \sin \alpha(\sin OP \cos \theta_1 - \cos OP \sin \theta_1);$$
$$\sin x_2 = \sin \alpha \sin OP_2 = \sin \alpha \sin(OP + \theta_2)$$
$$= \sin \alpha(\sin OP \cos \theta_2 + \cos OP \sin \theta_2).$$

Multiply the former by $\sin \theta_2$, and the latter by $\sin \theta_1$, and add; thus

$$\sin \theta_2 \sin x_1 + \sin \theta_1 \sin x_2 = \sin(\theta_1 + \theta_2)\sin \alpha \sin OP$$
$$= \sin(\theta_1 + \theta_2)\sin x.$$

The student should convince himself by examination that the result holds for all relative positions of P, P_1 and P_2, when due regard is paid to algebraical signs.

138. The principal use of Art. 137 is to determine whether three given points are on the same great circle; an illustration will be given in Art. 146.

139. *The arcs drawn from the angles of a spherical triangle perpendicular to the opposite sides respectively meet at a point.*

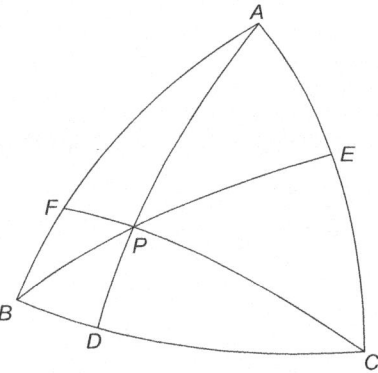

Let *CF* be perpendicular to *AB*. From *F* suppose arcs drawn perpendicular to *CB* and *CA* respectively; denote the former by ξ and the latter by η. Then, by Art. 135,

$$\frac{\sin \xi}{\sin \eta} = \frac{\sin FCB}{\sin FCA}.$$

But, by Art. 65,

$$\cos B = \cos CF \sin FCB, \cos A = \cos CF \sin FCA;$$

therefore
$$\frac{\sin \xi}{\sin \eta} = \frac{\cos B}{\cos A} = \frac{\cos B \cos C}{\cos A \cos C}.$$

And if from *any* point in *CF* arcs are drawn perpendicular to *CB* and *CA* respectively, the ratio of the sine of the former perpendicular to the sine of the latter perpendicular is equal to $\dfrac{\sin \xi}{\sin \eta}$ by Art. 135.

In like manner suppose *AD* perpendicular to *BC*; then if from any point in *AD* arcs are drawn perpendicular to *AC* and *AB* respectively, the ratio of the sine of the former perpendicular to the sine of the latter perpendicular is equal to $\dfrac{\cos A \cos C}{\cos A \cos B}$.

Let *CF* and *AD* meet at *P*, and from *P* let perpendiculars be drawn on the sides *a*, *b*, *c* of the triangle; and denote these perpendiculars by *x*, *y*, *z* respectively: then we have shewn that

$$\frac{\sin x}{\sin y} = \frac{\cos B \cos C}{\cos A \cos C},$$

and that
$$\frac{\sin y}{\sin z} = \frac{\cos A \cos C}{\cos A \cos B};$$

hence it follows that

$$\frac{\sin x}{\sin z} = \frac{\cos B \cos C}{\cos B \cos A},$$

and this shews that the point *P* is on the arc drawn from *B* perpendicular to *AC*.

Thus the three perpendiculars meet at a point, and this point is determined by the relations

$$\frac{\sin x}{\cos B \cos C} = \frac{\sin y}{\cos C \cos A} = \frac{\sin z}{\cos A \cos B}.$$

140. In the same manner it may be shewn that the arcs drawn from the angles of a spherical triangle to the middle points of the opposite sides meet at a point; and if from this point arcs x, y, z are drawn perpendicular to the sides a, b, c respectively,

$$\frac{\sin x}{\sin B \sin C} = \frac{\sin y}{\sin C \sin A} = \frac{\sin z}{\sin A \sin B}.$$

141. It is known in Plane Geometry that a certain circle touches the inscribed and escribed circles of any triangle; this circle is called the *Nine points circle: see Appendix to Euclid*, pages 317, 318, and *Plane Trigonometry*, Chapter 14.

We shall now shew that a small circle can always be determined on the sphere to touch the inscribed and escribed circles of any spherical triangle.

142. Let α denote the distance from A of the pole of the small circle inscribed within a spherical triangle ABC. Suppose that a small circle of angular radius ρ touches this inscribed circle internally; let β be the distance from A of the pole of this touching circle; let γ be the angle between arcs drawn from A to the pole of the inscribed circle and the pole of the touching circle respectively.

Then we must have

$$\cos(\rho - r) = \cos \alpha \cos \beta + \sin \alpha \sin \beta \cos \gamma. \qquad (1)$$

Suppose that this touching circle also touches externally the escribed circle of angular radius r_1; then if α_1 denote the distance from A of the pole of this escribed circle, we must have

$$\cos(\rho + r_1) = \cos\alpha_1 \cos\beta + \sin\alpha_1 \sin\beta \cos\gamma. \quad (2)$$

Similarly, if α_2 and α_3 denote the distances from A of the poles of the other escribed circles, in order that the touching circle may touch these escribed circles externally, we must also have

$$\cos(\rho + r_2) = \cos\alpha_2 \cos\beta + \sin\alpha_2 \sin\beta \cos\left(\frac{\pi}{2} - \gamma\right), \quad (3)$$

$$\cos(\rho + r_3) = \cos\alpha_3 \cos\beta + \sin\alpha_3 \sin\beta \cos\left(\frac{\pi}{2} + \gamma\right). \quad (4)$$

We shall shew that real values of ρ, β, and γ can be found to satisfy these four equations.

Eliminate $\cos\gamma$ from (1) and (2); thus

$$\cos\rho(\cos r\sin\alpha_1 - \cos r_1\sin\alpha) + \sin\rho(\sin r\sin\alpha_1 + \sin r_1\sin\alpha)$$
$$= \cos\beta(\cos\alpha\sin\alpha_1 - \cos\alpha_1\sin\alpha). \quad (5)$$

Suppose that the inscribed circle touches AB at the distance m from A, and that the escribed circle of angular radius r_1 touches AB at the distance m_1 from A. Then, by Art. 65,

$$\cot\alpha = \cot m\cos\frac{A}{2}, \cos\alpha = \cos r\cos m, \sin r = \sin\alpha\sin\frac{A}{2};$$

therefore $\quad \dfrac{\cos r}{\sin\alpha} = \dfrac{\cot\alpha}{\cos m} = \dfrac{1}{\sin m}\cos\dfrac{A}{2}.$

Similarly we may connect α_1 and r_1 with m_1. Thus we obtain from (5)

$$\cos \rho \cos \frac{A}{2}\left(\frac{1}{\sin m} - \frac{1}{\sin m_1}\right) + 2\sin \rho \sin \frac{A}{2}$$
$$= \cos \beta \cos \frac{A}{2}(\cot m - \cot m_1);$$

therefore $\cos \rho(\sin m_1 - \sin m) + 2\sin \rho \sin m \sin m_1 \tan \dfrac{A}{2}$
$$= \cos \beta \sin(m_1 - m).$$

But by Arts. 89 and 90 we have $m = s - a$, and $m_1 = s$; therefore by the aid of Art. 45 we obtain

$$2\cos \rho = \sin \frac{a}{2}\cos \frac{b+c}{2} + 2n\sin \rho = \cos \beta \sin a, \quad (6)$$

where n has the meaning assigned in Art. 46.

In like manner if we eliminate $\sin \gamma$ between (3) and (4), putting m_2 for $s - c$, and m_3 for $s - b$, we obtain

$$\cos \rho(\sin m_2 + \sin m_3) - 2\sin \rho \sin m_2 \sin m_3 \cot \frac{A}{2}$$
$$= \cos \beta \sin(m_2 + m_3),$$

therefore

$$2\cos \rho \sin \frac{a}{2}\cos \frac{b-c}{2} - 2n\sin \rho = \cos \beta \sin a. \quad (7)$$

From (6) and (7) we get

$$\tan \rho = \frac{\sin \frac{a}{2} \sin \frac{b}{2} \sin \frac{c}{2}}{n} = \frac{1}{2}\tan R, \text{ by Art. 92} \qquad (8)$$

and
$$\cos \beta = \frac{\cos \frac{b}{2} \cos \frac{c}{2} \cos \rho}{\cos \frac{a}{2}}. \qquad (9)$$

We may suppose that $\cos\dfrac{a}{2}$ is not less than $\cos\dfrac{b}{2}$ or $\cos\dfrac{c}{2}$, so that we are sure of a possible value of $\cos\beta$ from (9).

It remains to shew that when ρ and β are thus determined, all the four fundamental equations are satisfied.

It will be observed that, ρ and β being considered known, $\cos\gamma$ can be found from (1) or (2), and $\sin\gamma$ can be found from (3) or (4): we must therefore shew that (1) and (2) give the *same* value for $\cos\gamma$, and that (3) and (4) give the *same* value for $\sin\gamma$; and we must also shew that these values satisfy the condition $\cos^2\gamma + \sin^2\gamma = 1$.

From (1) we have

$$\frac{\cos\rho\sin r}{\sin\alpha}\left(\cos t + \tan\rho - \cos m \cot r\,\frac{\cos\beta}{\cos\rho}\right) = \sin\beta\cos\gamma,$$

that is,

$$\frac{\cos\rho\sin\frac{A}{2}}{n}\left\{\sin s + \sin\frac{1}{2}a\sin\frac{1}{2}b\sin\frac{1}{2}c - \frac{\cos(s-a)\sin s\cos\frac{b}{2}\cos\frac{c}{2}}{\cos\frac{a}{2}}\right\} = \sin\beta\cos\gamma;$$

this reduces to

$$\frac{\cos\rho\sin\frac{A}{2}}{n}\left\{\cos\frac{a}{2}\sin\frac{b+c}{2} - \frac{\sin(b+c)\cos\frac{b}{2}\cos\frac{c}{2}}{2\cos\frac{a}{2}}\right\}$$
$$= \sin\beta\cos\gamma:$$

and it will be found that (2) reduces to the same; so that (1) and (2) give the same value for cos γ.

In like manner it will be found that (3) and (4) agree in reducing to

$$\frac{\cos\rho\cos\frac{A}{2}}{n}\left\{\cos\frac{a}{2}\sin\frac{c-b}{2} - \frac{\sin(c-b)\cos\frac{b}{2}\cos\frac{c}{2}}{2\cos\frac{a}{2}}\right\}$$
$$= \sin\beta\cos\gamma.$$

It only remains to shew that the condition $\cos^2\gamma + \sin^2\gamma = 1$ is satisfied.

$$\text{Put } k \text{ for } \frac{\cos\beta}{\cos\rho}, \text{ that is for } \frac{\cos\frac{b}{2}\cos\frac{c}{2}}{\cos\frac{a}{2}};$$

put X for $\cot r\{1 - k\cos(s-a)\}$, and Y for $\cot r_1\{1 - k\cos s\}$.

Then (1) and (2) may be written respectively thus:

$$(X \cos \rho + \sin \rho) \sin \frac{A}{2} = \sin \beta \cos \gamma, \qquad (10)$$

$$(Y \cos \rho - \sin \rho) \sin \frac{A}{2} = \sin \beta \cos \gamma. \qquad (11)$$

From (10) and (11) by addition

$$(X + Y) \sin \frac{A}{2} \cos \rho = 2 \sin \beta \cos \gamma;$$

therefore

$$4 \sin^2 \beta \cos^2 \gamma = (X^2 + Y^2 + 2XY) \sin^2 \frac{A}{2} \cos^2 \rho. \quad (12)$$

But from (10) and (11) by subtraction

$$(X - Y) \cos \rho = -2 \sin \rho;$$

therefore

$$(X^2 + Y^2) \cos^2 \rho = 4 \sin^2 \rho + 2XY \cos^2 \rho.$$

Substitute in (12) and we obtain

$$\sin^2 \beta \cos^2 \gamma = (\sin^2 \rho + XY \cos^2 \rho) \sin^2 \frac{A}{2}. \qquad (13)$$

Again, put

X_1 for $\cot r_2 \{1 - k \cos(s - c)\}$, and Y_1 for $\cot r_3 \{1 - k \cos (s - b)\}$.

Then (3) and (4) may be written respectively thus:

$$(X_1 \cos \rho - \sin \rho)\cos \frac{A}{2} = \sin \beta \sin \gamma, \qquad (14)$$

$$(Y_1 \cos \rho - \sin \rho)\cos \frac{A}{2} = -\sin \beta \sin \gamma. \qquad (15)$$

From (14) and (15) by subtraction

$$(X_1 - Y_1)\cos \frac{A}{2}\cos \rho = 2 \sin \beta \sin \gamma,$$

and from (14) and (15) by addition,

$$(X_1 + Y_1)\cos \rho = 2 \sin \rho,$$

whence

$$\sin^2 \beta \sin^2 \gamma = \left(\sin^2 \rho - X_1 Y_1 \cos^2 \rho\right)\cos^2 \frac{A}{2}. \qquad (16)$$

Hence from (13) and (16) it follows that we have to establish the relation

$$\sin^2 \beta = \sin^2 \rho + \left(XY \sin^2 \frac{A}{2} - X_1 Y_1 \cos^2 \frac{A}{2}\right)\cos^2 \rho.$$

But $\sin^2 \beta = 1 - \cos^2 \beta = \sin^2 \rho + \cos^2 \rho - k^2 \cos^2 \rho$, so that the relation reduces to

$$1 - k^2 = XY \sin^2 \frac{A}{2} - X_1 Y_1 \cos^2 \frac{A}{2}.$$

Now

$$XY \sin^2 \frac{A}{2} = \frac{\cot r \cot r_1 \{1 - k \cos s\} \{1 - k \cos(s-a)\}}{\sin(s-b)\sin(s-c)}$$
$$= \frac{\{1 - k \cos s\} \{1 - k \cos(s-a)\}}{\sin b \sin c}.$$

Similarly

$$X_1 Y_1 \cos^2 \frac{A}{2} = \frac{\{1 - k \cos(s-b)\} \{1 - k \cos(s-c)\}}{\sin b \sin c}.$$

Subtract the latter from the former; then we obtain

$$\frac{k}{\sin b \sin c} \{\cos(s-b) + \cos(s-c) - \cos s - \cos(s-a)\}$$
$$+ \frac{k^2}{\sin b \sin c} \{\cos s \cos(s-a) - \cos(s-b)\cos(s-c)\},$$

that is

$$\frac{2k \cos \dfrac{a}{2}}{\sin b \sin c} \left\{ \cos \frac{b-c}{2} - \cos \frac{b+c}{2} \right\} + \frac{k^2}{\sin b \sin c}$$
$$\left\{ \cos \frac{b+c+a}{2} \cos \frac{b+c-a}{2} - \cos \frac{a+c-b}{2} \cos \frac{a+b-c}{2} \right\}$$

that is

$$\frac{4 \sin \frac{b}{2} \sin \frac{c}{2} \cos \frac{b}{2} \cos \frac{c}{2}}{\sin b \sin c} + \frac{k^2}{\sin b \sin c} \left\{ \sin^2 \frac{c-b}{2} - \sin^2 \frac{c+b}{2} \right\},$$

that is $1 - k^2$; which was to be shewn.

143. Thus the existence of a circle which touches the inscribed and escribed circles of any spherical triangle has been established.

The distance of the pole of this touching circle from the angles B and C of the triangle will of course be determined by formulæ corresponding to (9); and thus it follows that

$$\frac{\cos\frac{a}{2}\cos\frac{c}{2}\cos\rho}{\cos\frac{b}{2}} \text{ and } \frac{\cos\frac{a}{2}\cos\frac{b}{2}\cos\rho}{\cos\frac{c}{2}},$$

must both be less than unity.

144. Since the circle which has been determined touches the inscribed circle internally and touches the escribed circles externally, it is obvious that it must meet all the sides of the spherical triangle. We will now determine the position of the points of meeting.

Suppose the touching circle intersects the side AB at points distant λ and μ respectively from A.

Then by Art. 134 we have

$$\tan\frac{\lambda}{2}\tan\frac{\mu}{2} = \frac{\cos\rho - \cos\beta}{\cos\rho + \cos\beta} = \frac{\cos\frac{a}{2} - \cos\frac{b}{2}\cos\frac{c}{2}}{\cos\frac{a}{2} + \cos\frac{b}{2}\cos\frac{c}{2}}. \quad (1)$$

In the same way we must have by symmetry

$$\tan\frac{c-\lambda}{2}\tan\frac{c-\mu}{2} = \frac{\cos\frac{b}{2} - \cos\frac{a}{2}\cos\frac{c}{2}}{\cos\frac{b}{2} + \cos\frac{a}{2}\cos\frac{c}{2}}. \quad (2)$$

From (2), when we substitute the value of $\tan \dfrac{\lambda}{2} \tan \dfrac{\mu}{2}$ given by (1), we obtain

$$\tan \frac{\lambda}{2} + \tan \frac{\mu}{2} = \frac{\cos^2 \frac{a}{2} - \cos^2 \frac{b}{2} \cos^2 \frac{c}{2} + \cos^2 \frac{b}{2} \sin^2 \frac{c}{2}}{\cos \frac{b}{2} \sin \frac{c}{2} \left(\cos \frac{a}{2} + \cos \frac{b}{2} \cos \frac{c}{2}\right)}$$

$$= \frac{\cos \frac{a}{2} - \cos \frac{b}{2} \cos \frac{c}{2}}{\cos \frac{b}{2} \sin \frac{c}{2}} + \frac{\cos \frac{b}{2} \sin \frac{c}{2}}{\cos \frac{a}{2} + \cos \frac{b}{2} \cos \frac{c}{2}}. \tag{3}$$

From (1) and (3) we see that we may put

$$\tan \frac{\lambda}{2} = \frac{\cos \frac{a}{2} - \cos \frac{b}{2} \cos \frac{c}{2}}{\cos \frac{b}{2} \sin \frac{c}{2}}. \tag{4}$$

$$\tan \frac{\mu}{2} = \frac{\cos \frac{b}{2} \sin \frac{c}{2}}{\cos \frac{a}{2} + \cos \frac{b}{2} \cos \frac{c}{2}}. \tag{5}$$

Similar formulæ of course hold for the points of intersection of the touching circle with the other sides.

145. Let z denote the perpendicular from the pole of the touching circle on AB; then

$$\sin z = \sin \beta \sin\left(\frac{A}{2} + \gamma\right)$$

$$= \sin \beta \left(\sin \frac{A}{2} \cos \gamma + \cos \frac{A}{2} \sin \gamma\right).$$

But from (2) and (3) of Art. 142 we have

$$\sin \beta \cos \gamma = \frac{\cos \rho \sin \frac{A}{2}}{n} \left(Z - \sin \frac{a}{2} \sin \frac{b}{2} \sin \frac{c}{2}\right),$$

where $Z = \sin(s-a) - \cos s \sin(s-a) \cos \dfrac{b}{2} \cos \dfrac{c}{2} \sec \dfrac{a}{2}$,

and $\quad \sin \beta \sin \gamma = \dfrac{\cos \rho \cos \frac{A}{2}}{n} \left(Z_1 - \sin \dfrac{a}{2} \sin \dfrac{b}{2} \sin \dfrac{c}{2} \right)$,

where

$$Z_1 = \sin(s-b) - \cos(s-c)\sin(s-b)\cos\dfrac{b}{2}\cos\dfrac{c}{2}\sec\dfrac{a}{2}.$$

Therefore

$$\sin z - \dfrac{\cos \rho}{n}\left\{ Z \sin^2 \dfrac{A}{2} + Z_1 \cos^2 \dfrac{A}{2} - \sin\dfrac{a}{2}\sin\dfrac{b}{2}\sin\dfrac{c}{2} \right\}.$$

Now

$$Z \sin^2 \dfrac{A}{2} = \dfrac{\sin(s-a)\sin(s-b)\sin(s-c)}{\sin b \sin c}$$
$$\left\{ 1 - \cos s \cos\dfrac{b}{2}\cos\dfrac{c}{2}\sec\dfrac{a}{2} \right\},$$

and

$$Z_1 \cos^2 \dfrac{A}{2} = \dfrac{\sin s \sin(s-a)\sin(s-b)}{\sin b \sin c}$$
$$\left\{ 1 - \cos(s-c)\cos\dfrac{b}{2}\cos\dfrac{c}{2}\sec\dfrac{a}{2} \right\}.$$

Therefore

$$Z \sin^2 \frac{A}{2} + Z_1 \cos^2 \frac{A}{2}$$

is equal to the product of

$$\frac{\sin(s-a)\sin(s-b)}{\sin b \sin c}$$

into

$$\sin(s-c) + \sin s - \cos\frac{b}{2}\cos\frac{c}{2}\sec\frac{a}{2}\{\sin(s-c)\cos s + \cos(s-c)\sin s\}$$

$$= \frac{\sin(s-a)\sin(s-b)}{\sin b \sin c}\left\{2\sin\frac{a+b}{2}\cos\frac{c}{2} - \cos\frac{b}{2}\right.$$
$$\left.\cos\frac{c}{2}\sec\frac{a}{2}\sin(2s-c)\right\}$$

$$= \frac{\sin(s-a)\sin(s-b)}{2\sin b \sin\frac{c}{2}}\left\{2\sin\frac{a+b}{2} - \sin(a+b)\cos\frac{b}{2}\sec\frac{a}{2}\right\}$$

$$= \frac{\sin(s-a)\sin(s-b)\sin\frac{a+b}{2}}{\sin b \sin\frac{c}{2}}\left\{1 - \frac{\cos\frac{a+b}{2}\cos\frac{b}{2}}{\cos\frac{a}{2}}\right\}$$

$$= \frac{\sin(s-a)\sin(s-b)\sin^2\frac{a+b}{2}\sin\frac{b}{2}}{\sin b \sin\frac{c}{2}\cos\frac{a}{2}}$$

$$= \frac{\sin(s-a)\sin(s-b)\sin^2\frac{a+b}{2}}{2\cos\frac{a}{2}\cos\frac{b}{2}\sin\frac{c}{2}}.$$

Therefore

$$\sin z = \frac{\cos\rho}{n}\sin\frac{a}{2}\sin\frac{b}{2}\sin\frac{c}{2}\left\{\frac{2\sin^2\frac{a+b}{2}\sin(s-a)\sin(s-b)}{\sin^2\frac{c}{2}\sin a\sin b}-1\right\}$$

$$=\frac{\cos\rho}{n}\sin\frac{a}{2}\sin\frac{b}{2}\sin\frac{c}{2}\left\{2\cos^2\frac{A-B}{2}-1\right\};\text{ by (2) of Art. 54.}$$

Thus $\quad \sin z = \dfrac{\cos\rho}{n}\sin\dfrac{a}{2}\sin\dfrac{b}{2}\sin\dfrac{c}{2}\cos(A-B)$

$$=\sin\rho\cos(A-B).$$

Similar expressions hold for the perpendiculars from the pole of the touching circle on the other sides of the spherical triangle.

146. Let P denote the point determined in Art. 139; G the point determined in Art. 140, and N the pole of the touching circle. We shall now shew that P, G, and N are on a great circle.

Let x, y, z denote the perpendiculars from N on the sides a, b, c respectively of the spherical triangle; let x_1, y_1, z_1 denote the perpendiculars from P; and x_2, y_2, z_2 the perpendiculars from G. Then by Arts. 145, 139, and 140 we have

$$\frac{\sin x}{\cos(B-C)}=\frac{\sin y}{\cos(C-A)}=\frac{\sin z}{\cos(A-B)},$$

$$\frac{\sin x_1}{\cos B\cos C}=\frac{\sin y_1}{\cos C\cos A}=\frac{\sin z_1}{\cos A\cos B},$$

$$\frac{\sin x_2}{\sin B\sin C}=\frac{\sin y_2}{\sin C\sin A}=\frac{\sin y_3}{\sin A\sin B}.$$

Hence it follows that

$$\sin x = t_1 \sin x_1 + t_2 \sin x_2,$$
$$\sin y = t_1 \sin y_1 + t_2 \sin y_2,$$
$$\sin z = t_1 \sin z_1 + t_2 \sin z_2,$$

where t_1 and t_2 are certain quantities the values of which are not required for our purpose.

Therefore by Art. 137 a certain point *in the same great circle* as P and G is at the perpendicular distances x, y, z from the sides a, b, c respectively of the spherical triangle: and hence this point must be the point N.

147. The resemblance of the results which have been obtained to those which are known respecting the Nine points circle in Plane Geometry will be easily seen.

The result $\tan \rho = \dfrac{1}{2} \tan R$ corresponds to the fact that the radius of the Nine points circle is half the radius of the circumscribing circle of the triangle.

From equation (4) of Art. 144 by supposing the radius of the sphere to become infinite we obtain $\lambda = \dfrac{b^2 + c^2 - a^2}{2c}$: this corresponds to the fact that the Nine points circle passes through the feet of the perpendiculars from the angles of a triangle on the opposite sides.

From equation (5) of Art. 144 by supposing the radius of the sphere to become infinite we obtain $\mu = \dfrac{c}{2}$: this corresponds to the fact that the Nine points circle passes through the middle points of the sides of a triangle.

From Art. 145 by supposing the radius of the sphere to become infinite we obtain $z = \dfrac{1}{2}R\cos(A-B)$: this is a known property of the Nine points circle.

In Plane Geometry the points which correspond to the P, G, and N of Art. 146 are on a straight line.

148. The results which have been demonstrated with respect to the circle which touches the inscribed and escribed circles of a spherical triangle are mainly due to Dr Hart and Dr Salmon. See the *Quarterly Journal of Mathematics*, Vol. VI. page 67.

EXAMPLES

1. From the formula $\sin\dfrac{a}{2} = \sqrt{\left\{\dfrac{-\cos S\cos(S-A)}{\sin B\sin C}\right\}}$ deduce the expression for the area of a plane triangle, namely $\dfrac{a^2\sin B\sin C}{2\sin A}$, when the radius of the sphere is indefinitely increased.

2. Two triangles ABC, abc, spherical or plane, equal in all respects, differ slightly in position: shew that

$$\cos ABb \cos BCc \cos CAa + \cos ACc \cos CBb \cos BAa = 0.$$

3. Deduce formulæ in Plane Trigonometry from Napier's Analogies.

4. Deduce formulæ in Plane Trigonometry from Delambre's Analogies.

5. From the formula $\cos \dfrac{c}{2} \cos \dfrac{A+B}{2} = \sin \dfrac{C}{2} \cos \dfrac{a+b}{2}$ deduce the area of a plane triangle in terms of the sides and one of the angles.

6. What result is obtained from Example 7 to Chapter 6, by supposing the radius of the sphere infinite?

7. From the angle C of a spherical triangle a perpendicular is drawn to the arc which joins the middle points of the sides a and b: shew that this perpendicular makes an angle $S-B$ with the side a, and an angle $S-A$ with the side b.

8. From each angle of a spherical triangle a perpendicular is drawn to the arc which joins the middle points of the adjacent sides. Shew that these perpendiculars meet at a point; and that if x, y, z are the perpendiculars from this point on the sides a, b, c respectively,

$$\frac{\sin x}{\sin(S-B)\sin(S-C)} = \frac{\sin y}{\sin(S-C)\sin(S-A)}$$
$$= \frac{\sin z}{\sin(S-A)\sin(S-B)}.$$

9. Through each angle of a spherical triangle an arc is drawn so as to make the same angle with one side which the perpendicular on the base makes with the other side. Shew that these arcs meet at a point; and that if x, y, z are the perpendiculars from this point on the sides a, b, c respectively,

$$\frac{\sin x}{\cos A} = \frac{\sin y}{\cos B} = \frac{\sin z}{\cos C}.$$

10. Shew that the points determined in Examples 8 and 9, and the point N of Art. 146 are on a great circle.

State the corresponding theorem in Plane Geometry.

11. If one angle of a spherical triangle remains constant while the adjacent sides are increased, shew that the area and the sum of the angles are increased.

12. If the arcs bisecting two angles of a spherical triangle and terminated at the opposite sides are equal, the bisected angles will be equal provided their sum be less than $180°$.

[Let BOD and COE denote these two arcs which are given equal. If the angles B and C are not equal suppose B the greater. Then CD is greater than BE by Art. 58. And as the angle OBC is greater than the angle OCB, therefore OC is greater than OB; therefore OD is greater than OE. Hence the angle ODC is greater than the angle OEB, by Example 11. Then construct a spherical triangle BCF on the other side of BC, equal to CBE. Since the angle ODC is greater than the angle OEB, the angle FDC is greater than the angle DFC; therefore CD is less than CF, so that CD is less than BE. See the corresponding problem in Plane Geometry in the *Appendix to Euclid*, page 317.]

POLYHEDRONS

149. A polyhedron is a solid bounded by any number of plane rectilineal figures which are called its faces. A polyhedron is said to be *regular* when its faces are similar and equal regular polygons, and its solid angles equal to one another.

150. *If S be the number of solid angles in any polyhedron, F the number of its faces, E the number of its edges, then $S + F = E + 2$.*

Take any point within the polyhedron as centre, and describe a sphere of radius r, and draw straight lines from the centre to each of the angular points of the polyhedron; let the points at which these straight lines meet the surface of the sphere be joined by arcs of great circles, so that the surface of the sphere is divided into as many polygons as the polyhedron has faces.

Let s denote the sum of the angles of any one of these polygons, m the number of its sides; then the area of the polygon is $r^2\{s-(m-2)\pi\}$ by Art. 99. The sum of the areas of all the polygons is the surface of the sphere, that is, $4\pi r^2$. Hence since the number of the polygons is F, we obtain

$$4\pi - \Sigma s - \pi \Sigma m + 2F\pi.$$

Now Σs denotes the sum of all the angles of the polygons, and is therefore equal to $2\pi \times$ the number of solid angles, that is, to $2\pi S$; and Σm is equal to the number of all the sides of all the polygons, that is, to $2E$, since every edge gives rise to an arc which is common to two polygons. Therefore

$$4\pi = 2\pi S - 2\pi E + 2F\pi;$$

therefore $S + F = E + 2.$

151. *There can be only five regular polyhedrons.*

Let m be the number of sides in each face of a regular polyhedron, n the number of plane angles in each solid angle; then the entire number of plane angles is expressed by mF, or by nS, or by $2E$; thus

$$mF = nS = 2E, \text{ and } S + F = E + 2;$$

from these equations we obtain

$$S = \frac{4m}{2(m+n)-mn}, E = \frac{2mn}{2(m+n)-mn}, F = \frac{4n}{2(m+n)-mn}.$$

These expressions must be positive integers, we must therefore have $2(m+n)$ greater than mn; therefore

$$\frac{1}{m} + \frac{1}{n} \text{ must be greater than } \frac{1}{2};$$

but *n* cannot be less than 3, so that $\frac{1}{n}$ cannot be greater than $\frac{1}{3}$, and therefore $\frac{1}{m}$ must be greater than $\frac{1}{6}$; and as *m* must be an integer and cannot be less than 3, the only admissible values of *m* are 3, 4, 5. It will be found on trial that the only values of *m* and *n* which satisfy all the necessary conditions are the following: each regular polyhedron derives its name from the number of its plane faces.

m	*n*	*S*	*E*	*F*	Name of regular polyhedron
3	3	4	6	4	Tetrahedron or regular pyramid
4	3	8	12	6	Hxahedron or cube
3	4	6	12	8	Octrahedron
5	3	20	30	12	Dodecahedron
3	5	12	30	20	Icosahedron

It will be seen that the demonstration establishes something more than the enunciation states; for it is not assumed that the faces are equilateral and equiangular and all equal. It is in fact demonstrated that, *there cannot be more than five solids each of which has all its faces with the same number of sides, and all its solid angles formed with the same number of plane angles.*

152. *The sum of all the plane angles which form the solid angles of any polyhedron is* $2(S-2)\pi.$

For if *m* denote the number of sides in any face of the polyhedron, the sum of the interior angles of that face is $(m-2)\pi$ by Euclid I. 32, Cor. 1. Hence the sum of all the interior angles of all the faces is $\Sigma(m-2)\pi$, that is $\Sigma m\pi - 2F\pi$, that is $2(E-F)\pi$, that is $2(S-2)\pi$.

153. *To find the inclination of two adjacent faces of a regular polyhedron.*

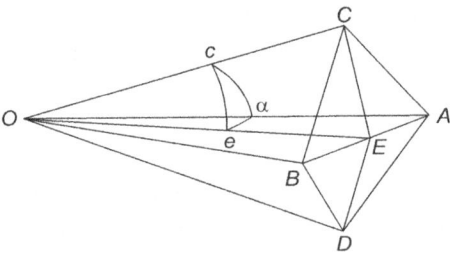

Let *AB* be the edge common to the two adjacent faces, *C* and *D* the centres of the faces; bisect *AB* at *E*, and join *CE* and *DE*; *CE* and *DE* will be perpendicular to *AB*, and the angle *CED* is the angle of inclination of the two adjacent faces; we shall denote it by *I*. In the plane containing *CE* and *DE* draw *CO* and *DO* at right angles to *CE* and *DE* respectively, and meeting at *O*; about *O* as centre describe a sphere meeting *OA*, *OC*, *OE* at *a*, *c*, e respectively, so that *cae* forms a spherical triangle. Since *AB* is perpendicular to *CE* and *DE*, it is perpendicular to the plane *CED*, therefore the plane *AOB* which contains *AB* is perpendicular to the plane *CED*; hence the angle *cea* of the spherical triangle is a right angle. Let *m* be the number of sides in each face of the polyhedron, *n* the number of the plane angles which form

each solid angle. Then the angle $ace = ACE = \dfrac{2\pi}{2m} = \dfrac{\pi}{m}$;
and the angle cae is half one of the n equal angles formed on
the sphere round a, that is, $cae = \dfrac{2\pi}{2n} = \dfrac{\pi}{n}$. From the right-
angled triangle cae

$$\cos cae = \cos cOe \sin ace,$$

that is $\qquad \cos\dfrac{\pi}{n} = \cos\left(\dfrac{\pi}{2} - \dfrac{I}{2}\right)\sin\dfrac{\pi}{m};$

therefore $\qquad \sin\dfrac{I}{2} = \dfrac{\cos\frac{\pi}{n}}{\sin\frac{\pi}{m}}.$

154. *To find the radii of the inscribed and circumscribed*
spheres of a regular polyhedron.

Let the edge $AB = a$, let $OC = r$ and $OA = R$, so that r is the
radius of the inscribed sphere, and R is the radius of the
circumscribed sphere. Then

$$CE = AE \cot ACE = \dfrac{a}{2}\cot\dfrac{\pi}{m},$$

$$r = CE \tan CEO = CE \tan\dfrac{I}{2} = \dfrac{a}{2}\cot\dfrac{\pi}{m}\tan\dfrac{I}{2};$$

also $\quad r = R\cos aOc = R\cot eca\cot eac = R\cot\dfrac{\pi}{m}\cot\dfrac{\pi}{n};$

therefore $\quad R = r\tan\dfrac{\pi}{m}\tan\dfrac{\pi}{n} = \dfrac{a}{2}\tan\dfrac{I}{2}\tan\dfrac{\pi}{n}.$

155. *To find the surface and volume of a regular polyhedron.*

The area of one face of the polyhedron is $\dfrac{ma^2}{4}\cot\dfrac{\pi}{m}$, and

therefore the surface of the polyhedron is $\dfrac{mFa^2}{4}\cot\dfrac{\pi}{m}$.

Also the volume of the pyramid which has one face of the

polyhedron for base and O for vertex is $\dfrac{r}{3}.\dfrac{ma^2}{4}\cot\dfrac{\pi}{m}$, and

therefore the volume of the polyhedron is $\dfrac{mFra^2}{12}\cot\dfrac{\pi}{m}$.

156. *To find the volume of a parallelepiped in terms of its edges and their inclinations to one another.*

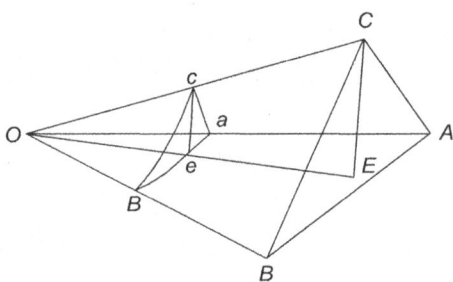

Let the edges be $OA = a$, $OB = b$, $OC = c$; let the inclinations be $BOC = a$, $COA = \beta$, $AOB = \gamma$. Draw CE perpendicular to the plane AOB meeting it at E. Describe a sphere with O as a centre, meeting OA, OB, OC, OE at a, b, c, e respectively.

The volume of the parallelepiped is equal to the product of its base and altitude $= ab \sin \gamma$. $CE = abc \sin \gamma \sin cOe$. The spherical triangle cae is right-angled at e; thus

$$\sin cOe = \sin cOa \sin cae = \sin \beta \sin cab,$$

and from the spherical triangle cab

$$\sin cab = \frac{\sqrt{\left(1 - \cos^2 \alpha - \cos^2 \beta - \cos^2 \gamma + 2 \cos \alpha \cos \beta \cos \gamma\right)}}{\sin \beta \sin \gamma};$$

therefore the volume of the parallelepiped

$$= abc \sqrt{\left(1 - \cos^2 \alpha - \cos^2 \beta - \cos^2 \gamma + 2 \cos \alpha \cos \beta \cos \gamma\right)}.$$

157. *To find the diagonal of a parallelepiped in terms of the three edges which it meets and their inclinations to one another.*

Let the edges be $OA = a$, $OB = b$, $OC = c$; let the inclinations be $BOC = \alpha$, $COA = \beta$, $AOB = \gamma$. Let OD be the diagonal required, and let OE be the diagonal of the face OAB. Then

$$OD^2 = OE^2 + ED^2 + 2OE.ED \cos COE$$
$$= a^2 + b^2 + 2ab \cos \gamma + c^2 + 2cOE \cos COE.$$

Describe a sphere with O as centre meeting OA, OB, OC, OE at a, b, c, e respectively; then (see Example 14, Chapter 4.)

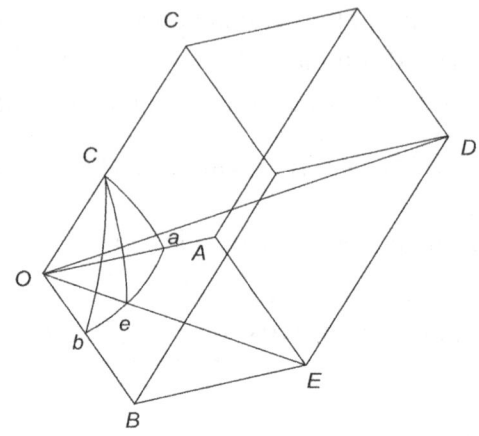

$$\cos cOe = \frac{\cos cOb \sin aOe + \cos cOa \sin bOe}{\sin aOb}$$

$$= \frac{\cos \alpha \sin aOe + \cos \beta \sin bOe}{\sin \gamma};$$

therefore

$$OD^2 = a^2 + b^2 + c^2 + 2ab \cos \gamma + \frac{2cOE}{\sin \gamma}$$
$$(\cos \alpha \sin aOe + \cos \beta \sin bOe),$$

and $OE \sin aOe = b \sin \gamma,$ $OE \sin bOe = a \sin \gamma;$

therefore

$$OD^2 = a^2 + b^2 + c^2 + 2ab \cos \gamma + 2bc \cos \alpha + 2ca \cos \beta.$$

158. *To find the volume of a tetrahedron.*

A tetrahedron is one-sixth of a parallelepiped which has the same altitude and its base double that of the tetrahedron; thus if the edges and their inclinations are given we can take one-sixth of the expression for the volume in Art. 156. The volume of a tetrahedron may also be expressed in terms of its six edges; for in the figure of Art. 156 let $BC = a'$, $CA = b'$, $AB = c'$; then

$$\cos \alpha = \frac{b^2 + c^2 - a'^2}{2bc}, \cos \beta = \frac{c^2 + a^2 - b'^2}{2ca},$$

$$\cos \gamma = \frac{a^2 + b^2 - c'^2}{2ab},$$

and if these values are substituted for cos α, cos β, cos γ in the expression obtained in Art. 156, the volume of the tetrahedron will be expressed in terms of its six edges.

The following result will be obtained, in which V denotes the volume of the tetrahedron,

$$144V^2 = -a'^2 b'^2 c'^2 + a^2 a'^2 (b'^2 + c'^2 - a'^2) +$$
$$b^2 b'^2 (c'^2 + a'^2 - b'^2) + c'^2 (a'^2 + b'^2 - c'^2) -$$
$$a'^2 (a^2 - b^2)(a^2 - c^2) - b'^2 (b^2 - c^2)(b^2 - a^2) -$$
$$c'^2 (c^2 - a^2)(c^2 - b^2).$$

Thus for a *regular* tetrahedron we have $144V^2 = 2a^6$.

159. If the vertex of a tetrahedron be supposed to be situated at any point in the plane of its base, the volume vanishes; hence if we equate to zero the expression on the right-hand side of the equation just given, we obtain a relation which must hold among the six straight lines which join four points taken arbitrarily in a plane.

Or we may adopt Carnot's method, in which this relation is established independently, and the expression for the volume of a tetrahedron is deduced from it; this we shall now shew, and we shall add some other investigations which are also given by Carnot.

It will be convenient to alter the notation hitherto used, by interchanging the accented and unaccented letters.

160. *To find the relation holding among the six straight lines which join four points taken arbitrarily in a plane.*

Let *A*, *B*, *C*, *D* be the four points. Let $AB = c$, $BC = a$, $CA = b$; also let $DA = a'$, $DB = b'$, $DC = c'$.

If *D* falls *within* the triangle *ABC*, the sum of the angles *ADB*, *BDC*, *CDA* is equal to four right angles; so that

$$\cos ADB = \cos (BDC + CDA).$$

Hence by ordinary transformations we deduce

$$1 = \cos^2 ADB + \cos^2 BDC + \cos^2 CDA - 2 \cos ADB \cos BDC \cos CDA.$$

If *D* falls *without* the triangle *ABC*, one of the three angles at *D* is equal to the sum of the other two, and the result just given still holds.

Now $\cos ADB = \dfrac{a'^2 + b'^2 - c^2}{2a'b'}$, and the other cosines may be expressed in a similar manner; substitute these values in the above result, and we obtain the required relation, which after reduction may be exhibited thus,

$$0 = -a^2b^2c^2 + a'^2a^2(b^2 + c^2 - a^2) + b'^2b^2(c^2 + a^2 - b^2)$$
$$+ c'^2c^2(a^2 + b^2 - c^2) - a^2(a'^2 - b'^2)(a'^2 - c'^2) -$$
$$b^2(b'^2 - c'^2)(b'^2 - a'^2) - c^2(c'^2 - a'^2)(c'^2 - b'^2).$$

161. *To express the volume of a tetrahedron in terms of its six edges.*

Let a, b, c be the lengths of the sides of a triangle ABC forming one face of the tetrahedron, which we may call its base; let a', b', c' be the lengths of the straight lines which join A, B, C respectively to the vertex of the tetrahedron.

Let p be the length of the perpendicular from the vertex on the base; then the lengths of the straight lines drawn from the foot of the perpendicular to A, B, C respectively are $\sqrt{(a'^2 - p^2)}, \sqrt{(b'^2 - p^2)}, \sqrt{(c'^2 - p^2)}$. Hence the relation given in Art. 160 will hold if we put $\sqrt{(a'^2 - p^2)}$ instead of a', $\sqrt{(b'^2 - p^2)}$ instead of b', and $\sqrt{(c'^2 - p^2)}$ instead of c'. We shall thus obtain

$$p^2(2a^2b^2 + 2b^2c^2 + 2c^2a^2 - a^4 - b^4 - c^4) = -a^2b^2c^2$$
$$+ a'^2a^2(b^2 + c^2 - a^2) + b'^2b^2(c^2 + a^2 - b^2)$$
$$+ c'^2c^2(a^2 + b^2 - c^2) - a^2(a'^2 - b'^2)(a'^2 - c'^2)$$
$$- b^2(b'^2 - c'^2)(b'^2 - a'^2) - c^2(c'^2 - a'^2)(c'^2 - b'^2).$$

The coefficient of p^2 in this equation is sixteen times the square of the area of the triangle ABC; so that the left-hand member is $144\,V^2$, where V denotes the volume of the tetrahedron. Hence the required expression is obtained.

162. *To find the relation holding among the six arcs of great circles which join four points taken arbitrarily on the surface of a sphere.*

Let A, B, C, D be the four points. Let $AB = \gamma$, $BC = \alpha$, $CA = \beta$; let $DA = \alpha'$, $DB = \beta'$, $DC = \gamma'$.

As in Art. 160 we have

$$1 = \cos^2 ADE + \cos^2 BDC + \cos^2 CDA - 2\cos ADB \; \cos BDC \cos CDA.$$

Now $\cos ADB = \dfrac{\cos \gamma - \cos \alpha' \cos \beta'}{\sin \alpha' \sin \beta'}$, and the other cosines may be expressed in a similar manner; substitute these values in the above result, and we obtain the required relation, which after reduction may be exhibited thus,

$$\begin{aligned}
1 =\ & \cos^2 \alpha + \cos^2 \beta + \cos^2 \gamma + \cos^2 \alpha' + \cos^2 \beta' + \cos^2 \gamma' \\
& - \cos^2 \alpha \cos^2 \alpha' - \cos^2 \beta \cos^2 \beta' - \cos^2 \gamma \cos^2 \gamma' \\
& - 2(\cos \alpha \cos \beta \cos \gamma + \cos \alpha \cos \beta' \cos \gamma' \\
& + \cos \beta \cos \alpha' \cos \gamma' + \cos \gamma \cos \alpha' \cos \beta') \\
& + 2(\cos \alpha \cos \beta \cos \alpha' \cos \beta' + \cos \beta \cos \gamma \cos \beta' \cos \gamma' \\
& + \cos \gamma \cos \alpha \cos \gamma' \cos \alpha').
\end{aligned}$$

163. *To find the radius of the sphere circumscribing a tetrahedron.*

Denote the edges of the tetrahedron as in Art. 161. Let the sphere be supposed to be circumscribed about the tetrahedron, and draw on the sphere the six arcs of great circles joining the angular points of the tetrahedron. Then the relation given in Art. 162 holds among the cosines of these six arcs.

Let r denote the radius of the sphere. Then

$$\cos \alpha = 1 - 2\sin^2 \frac{\alpha}{2} = 1 - 2\left(\frac{a}{2r}\right)^2 = 1 - \frac{a^2}{2r^2};$$

and the other cosines may be expressed in a similar manner. Substitute these values in the result of Art. 162, and we obtain, after reduction, with the aid of Art. 161,

$$4 \times 144 V^2 r^2 = 2a^2 b^2 a'^2 b'^2 + 2b^2 c^2 b'^2 c'^2$$
$$+ 2c^2 a^2 c'^2 a'^2 - a^4 a'^4 - b^4 b'^4 - c^4 c'^4.$$

The right-hand member may also be put into factors, as we see by recollecting the mode in which the expression for the area of a triangle is put into factors.

Let $aa' + bb' + cc' = 2\sigma$; then

$$36V^2 r^2 = \sigma(\sigma - aa')(\sigma - bb')(\sigma - cc').$$

EXAMPLES

1. If I denote the inclination of two adjacent faces of a regular polyhedron, shew that $\cos I = \dfrac{1}{3}$ in the tetrahedron, $= 0$ in the cube, $= -\dfrac{1}{3}$ in the octahedron, $= -\dfrac{1}{5}\sqrt{5}$ in the dodecahedron, and $= -\dfrac{1}{3}\sqrt{5}$ in the icosahedron.

2. With the notation of Art. 153, shew that the radius of the sphere which touches one face of a regular polyhedron and all the adjacent faces produced is $\dfrac{1}{2}a\cot\dfrac{\pi}{m}\cot\dfrac{1}{2}I$.

3. A sphere touches one face of a regular tetrahedron and the other three faces produced: find its radius.

4. If a and b are the radii of the spheres inscribed in and described about a regular tetrahedron, shew that $b = 3a$.

5. If a is the radius of a sphere inscribed in a regular tetrahedron, and R the radius of the sphere which touches the edges, shew that $R^2 = 3a^2$.

6. If a is the radius of a sphere inscribed in a regular tetrahedron, and R' the radius of the sphere which touches one face and the others produced, shew that $R' = 2a$.

7. If a cube and an octahedron be described about a given sphere, the sphere described about these polyhedrons will be the same; and conversely.

8. If a dodecahedron and an icosahedron be described about a given sphere, the sphere described about these polyhedrons will be the same; and conversely.

9. A regular tetrahedron and a regular octahedron are inscribed in the same sphere: compare the radii of the spheres which can be inscribed in the two solids.

10. The sum of the squares of the four diagonals of a parallelepiped is equal to four times the sum of the squares of the edges.

11. If with all the angular points of any parallelepiped as centres equal spheres be described, the sum of the intercepted portions of the parallelepiped will be equal in volume to one of the spheres.

12. A regular octahedron is inscribed in a cube so that the corners of the octahedron are at the centres of the faces of the cube: shew that the volume of the cube is six times that of the octahedron.

13. It is not possible to fill any given space with a number of regular polyhedrons of the same kind, except cubes; but this may be done by means of tetrahedrons and octahedrons which have equal faces, by using twice as many of the former as of the latter.

14. A spherical triangle is formed on the surface of a sphere of radius ρ; its angular points are joined, forming thus a pyramid with the straight lines joining them with the centre: shew that the volume of the pyramid is

$$\frac{1}{3}\rho^3 \sqrt{(\tan r \tan r_1 \tan r_2 \tan r_3)},$$

where r, r_1, r_2, r_3 are the radii of the inscribed and escribed circles of the triangle.

15. The angular points of a regular tetrahedron inscribed in a sphere of radius r being taken as poles, four equal small circles of the sphere are described, so that each circle touches the other three. Shew that the area of the surface bounded by each circle is $2\pi r^2 \left(1 - \dfrac{1}{\sqrt{3}}\right)$.

16. If O be any point within a spherical triangle ABC, the product of the sines of any two sides and the sine of the included angle

$$= \sin AO \sin BO \sin CO \{\cot AO \sin BOC$$
$$+ \cot BO \sin COA + \cot CO \sin AOB\}.$$

ARCS DRAWN TO FIXED POINTS ON THE SURFACE OF A SPHERE

164. In the present Chapter we shall demonstrate various propositions relating to the arcs drawn from any point on the surface of a sphere to certain fixed points on the surface.

165. *ABC* is a spherical triangle having all its sides quadrants, and therefore all its angles right angles; *T* is any point on the surface of the sphere: to shew that

$$\cos^2 TA + \cos^2 TB + \cos^2 TC = 1.$$

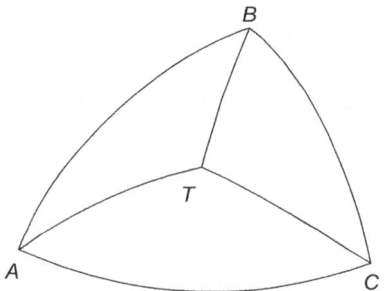

By Art. 37 we have

$$\cos TA = \cos AB \cos TB + \sin AB \sin TB \cos TBA$$
$$= \sin TB \cos TBA.$$

Similarly $\cos TC = \sin TB \cos TBC = \sin TB \sin TBA$. Square and add; thus

$$\cos^2 TA + \cos^2 TC = \sin^2 TB = 1 - \cos^2 TB;$$

therefore $\quad \cos^2 TA + \cos^2 TB + \cos^2 TC = 1$.

166. *ABC* is a spherical triangle having all its sides quadrants, and therefore all its angles right angles; *T* and *U* are any points on the surface of the sphere: to shew that

$$\cos TU = \cos TA \cos UA + \cos TB \cos UB + \cos TC \cos UC.$$

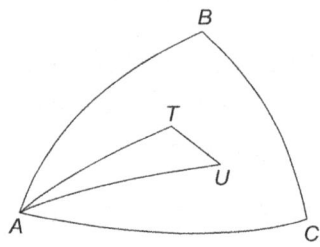

By Art. 37 we have

$$\cos TU = \cos TA \cos UA + \sin TA \sin UA \cos TAU,$$

and $\qquad \cos TAU = \cos(BAU - BAT)$

$$= \cos BAU \cos BAT + \sin BAU \sin BAT$$

$$= \cos BAU \cos BAT + \cos CAU \cos CAT;$$

therefore

$$\cos\ TU = \cos\ TA \cos\ UA + \sin\ TA \sin\ UA(\cos\ BAU$$
$$\cos\ BAT + \cos\ CAU \cos\ CAT\ );$$

and $\qquad \cos\ TB = \sin\ TA \cos\ BAT,$

$$\cos\ UB = \sin\ UA \cos\ BAU,$$

$$\cos\ TC = \sin\ TA \cos\ CAT,$$

$$\cos\ UC = \sin\ UA \cos\ CAU;$$

therefore

$$\cos\ TU = \cos\ TA \cos\ UA + \cos\ TB \cos\ UB + \cos\ TC \cos\ UC.$$

167. We leave to the student the exercise of shewing that the formulæ of the two preceding Articles are perfectly general for all positions of T and U, outside or inside the triangle ABC: the demonstrations will remain essentially the same for all modifications of the diagrams. The formulæ are of constant application in Analytical Geometry of three dimensions, and are demonstrated in works on that subject; we have given them here as they may be of service in Spherical Trigonometry, and will in fact now be used in obtaining some important results.

168. Let there be any number of fixed points on the surface of a sphere; denote them by $H_1, H_2, H_3,....$ Let T be any point on the surface of a sphere. We shall now investigate an expression for the sum of the cosines of the arcs which join T with the fixed points.

Denote the sum by Σ; so that

$$\Sigma = \cos TH_1 + \cos TH_2 + \cos TH_3 + \ldots.$$

Take on the surface of the sphere a fixed spherical triangle *ABC*, having all its sides quadrants, and therefore all its angles right angles.

Let λ, μ, ν be the cosines of the arcs which join *T* with *A*, *B*, *C* respectively; let l_1, m_1, n_1 be the cosines of the arcs which join H_1 with *A*, *B*, *C* respectively; and let a similar notation be used with respect to $H_2, H_3, \ldots$.

Then, by Art. 166,

$$\Sigma = l_1 \lambda + m_1 \mu + n_1 \nu + l_2 \lambda m_2 \mu + n_2 \nu + \ldots$$
$$= P\lambda + Q\mu + R\nu;$$

where *P* stands for $l_1 + l_2 + l_3 + \ldots$, with corresponding meanings for *Q* and *R*.

169. It will be seen that *P* is the value which Σ takes when *T* coincides with *A*, that *Q* is the value which Σ takes when *T* coincides with *B*, and that *R* is the value which Σ takes when *T* coincides with *C*. Hence the result expresses the general value of Σ in terms of the cosines of the arcs which join *T* to the fixed points *A*, *B*, *C*, and the particular values of Σ which correspond to these three points.

170. We shall now transform the result of Art. 168.

Let $\qquad G = \sqrt{\left(P^2 + Q^2 + R^2\right)};$

and let α, β, γ, be three arcs determined by the equations

$$\cos\alpha = \frac{P}{G}, \cos\beta = \frac{Q}{G}, \cos\gamma = \frac{R}{G};$$

then $\qquad \Sigma = G(\lambda\cos\alpha + \mu\cos\beta + \nu\cos\gamma).$

Since $\cos^2\alpha + \cos^2\beta + \cos^2\gamma = 1$, it is obvious that there will be some point on the surface of the sphere, such that α, β, γ are the arcs which join it to A, B, C respectively; denote this point by U: then, by Art. 166,

$$\cos TU = \lambda\cos\alpha + \mu\cos\beta + \nu\cos\gamma;$$

and finally

$$\Sigma = G\cos TU.$$

Thus, whatever may be the position of T, the sum of the cosines of the arcs which join T to the fixed points varies as the cosine of the single arc which joins T to a certain fixed point U.

We might take G either positive or negative; it will be convenient to suppose it positive.

171. A sphere is described about a regular polyhedron; from any point on the surface of the sphere arcs are drawn to the solid angles of the polyhedron: to shew that the sum of the cosines of these arcs is zero.

From the preceding Article we see that if G is not zero there is *one* position of T which gives to Σ its greatest positive value, namely, when T coincides with U. But by the symmetry of a regular polyhedron there must always be *more than one* position of T which gives the same value to Σ. For instance, if we take a regular tetrahedron, as there are four faces there will at least be *three other* positions of T symmetrical with any assigned position.

Hence G must be zero; and thus the *sum of the cosines of the arcs which join T to the solid angles of the regular polyhedron is zero for all positions of T.*

172. Since $G = 0$, it follows that P, Q, R must each be zero; these indeed are particular cases of the general result of Art. 171. See Art. 169.

173. The result obtained in Art. 171 may be shewn to hold also in some other cases. Suppose, for instance, that a rectangular parallelepiped is inscribed in a sphere; then the sum of the cosines of the arcs drawn from any point on the surface of the sphere to the solid angles of the parallelepiped is zero. For here it is obvious that there must always be at least *one other* position of T symmetrical with any assigned position. Hence by the argument of Art. 171 we must have $G = 0$.

174. Let there be any number of fixed points on the surface of a sphere; denote them by $H_1, H_2, H_3,...$ Let T be any point on the surface of the sphere. We shall now investigate a remarkable expression for the sum of the squares of the cosines of the arcs which join T with the fixed points.

Denote the sum by Σ; so that

$$\Sigma = \cos^2 TH_1 + \cos^2 TH_2 + \cos^2 TH_3 + \ ....$$

Take on the surface of the sphere a fixed spherical triangle *ABC*, having all its sides quadrants, and therefore all its angles right angles.

Let λ, μ, ν be the cosines of the arcs which join *T* with *A*, *B*, *C* respectively; let l_1, m_1, n_1 be the cosines of the angles which join H_1 with *A*, *B*, *C* respectively; and let a similar notation be used with respect to $H_2, H_3, \dots$.

Then, by Art. 166,

$$\Sigma = \left(l_1\lambda + m_1\mu + n_1\nu\right)^2 + \left(l_2\lambda + m_2\mu + n_2\nu\right)^2 + \dots.$$

Expand each square, and rearrange the terms; thus

$$\Sigma = P\lambda^2 + Q\mu^2 + R\nu^2 + 2p\mu\nu + 2q\nu\lambda + 2r\lambda\mu,$$
where *P* stands for $l_1^2 + l_2^2 + l_3^2 + \dots$,
and *p* stands for $m_1 n_1 + m_2 n_2 + m_3 n_3 + \dots$,

with corresponding meanings for *Q* and *q*, and for *R* and *r*.

We shall now shew that there is some position of the triangle *ABC* for which *p*, *q*, and *r* will vanish; so that we shall then have

$$\Sigma = P\lambda^2 + Q\mu^2 + R\nu^2.$$

Since Σ is always a finite positive quantity there must be some position, or some positions, of *T* for which Σ has the largest value which it can receive.

Suppose that A has this position, or one of these positions if there are more than one. When T is at A we have μ and ν each zero, and λ equal to unity, so that Σ is then equal to P.

Hence, whatever be the position of T, P is never less than $P\lambda^2 + Q\mu^2 + R\nu^2 + 2p\mu\nu + 2q\nu\lambda + 2r\lambda\mu$, that is, by Art. 165,

$$P(\lambda^2 + \mu^2 + \nu^2) \text{ is never less than}$$
$$P\lambda^2 + Q\mu^2 + R\nu^2 + 2p\mu\nu + 2q\nu\lambda + 2r\lambda\mu;$$

therefore

$$(P-Q)\mu^2 + (P-R)\nu^2 \text{ is never less than } 2p\mu\nu + 2q\nu\lambda + 2r\lambda\mu.$$

Now suppose $\nu = 0$; then T is situated on the great circle of which AB is a quadrant, and whatever be the position of T we have

$$(P-Q)\mu^2 \text{ not less than } 2r\lambda\mu,$$

and therefore $(P-Q)$ not less than $\dfrac{2r\lambda}{\mu}$.

But now $\dfrac{\lambda}{\mu}$ is equal to $\dfrac{\cos TA}{\cos TB}$; this is numerically equal to $\tan TB$, and so made numerically as great as we please, positive or negative, by giving a suitable position to T. Thus $P-Q$ must in some cases be less than $\dfrac{2r\lambda}{\mu}$ if r have any value different from zero.

Therefore r must $= 0$.

In like manner we can shew that q must $= 0$.

Hence with the specified position for A we arrive at the result that whatever may be the position of T

$$\Sigma = P\lambda^2 + Q\mu^2 + R\nu^2 + 2p\mu\nu.$$

Let us now suppose that the position of B is so taken that when T coincides with B the value of Σ is as large as it can be for any point in the great circle of which A is the pole. When T is at B we have λ and ν each zero, and μ equal to unity, so that Σ is then equal to Q. For any point in the great circle of which A is the pole λ is zero; and therefore for any such point

Q is not less than $Q\mu^2 + R\nu^2 + 2p\mu\nu$,

that is, by Art. 165,

$$Q\left(\mu^2 + \nu^2\right) \text{ is not less than } Q\mu^2 + R\nu^2 + 2p\mu\nu;$$

therefore $Q - R$ is not less than $\dfrac{2p\mu}{\nu}$.

Hence by the same reasoning as before we must have $p = 0$. Therefore we see that there must be some position of the triangle ABC, such that for every position of T

$$\Sigma = P\lambda^2 + Q\mu^2 + R\nu^2.$$

175. The remarks of Art. 169 are applicable to the result just obtained.

176. In the final result of Art. 174 we may shew that R is the least value which Σ can receive. For, by Art. 165,

$$\Sigma = P\lambda^2 + Q\mu^2 + R(1 - \lambda^2 - \mu^2)$$
$$= R + (P - R)\lambda^2 + (Q - R)\mu^2;$$

and by supposition neither $P - R$ nor $Q - R$ is negative, so that Σ cannot be less than R.

177. A sphere is described about a regular polyhedron; from any point on the surface of the sphere arcs are drawn to the solid angles of the polyhedron: it is required to find the sum of the squares of the cosines of these arcs.

With the notation of Art. 174 we have

$$\Sigma = P\lambda^2 + Q\mu^2 + R\nu^2.$$

We shall shew that in the present case P, Q, and R must *all be equal*. For if they are not, one of them must be greater than each of the others, or one of them must be less than each of the others.

If possible let the former be the case; suppose that P is greater than Q, and greater than R.

Now　　$\Sigma = P(1 - \mu^2 - \nu^2) + Q\mu^2 + R\nu^2$

$$= P - (P - Q)\mu^2 - (P - R)\nu^2;$$

this shews that Σ is *always less than P* except when $\mu = 0$ and $\nu = 0$: that is Σ *is always less than P* except when T is at A, or at the point of the surface which is diametrically opposite to A. But by the symmetry of a regular polyhedron there must always be more than two positions of T which give the same value to Σ. For instance if we take a regular tetrahedron, as there are *four* faces there will be at least *three other* positions of T symmetrical with any assigned position. Hence P cannot be greater than Q and greater than R.

In the same way we can shew that one of the three P, Q, and R, cannot be less than each of the others.

Therefore $P = Q = R$; and therefore by Art. 165 for *every position* of T we have $\Sigma = P$.

Since $P = Q = R$ each of them $= \dfrac{1}{3}(P + Q + R)$

$$= \frac{1}{3}\left\{ l_1^2 + m_1^2 + n_1^2 + l_2^2 + m_2^2 + n_2^2 + ... \right\}$$

$$= \frac{S}{3}, \text{ by Art.165,}$$

where S is the number of the solid angles of the regular polyhedron.

Thus the sum of the squares of the cosines of the arcs which join any point on the surface of the sphere to the solid angles of the regular polyhedron is one third of the number of the solid angles.

178. Since $P = Q = R$ in the preceding Article, it will follow that when the fixed points of Art. 174 are the solid angles of a regular polyhedron, then for any position of the spherical triangle ABC we shall have $p = 0, q = 0, r = 0$.

For taking any position for the spherical triangle ABC we have

$$\Sigma = P\lambda^2 + Q\mu^2 + R\nu^2 + 2p\mu\nu + 2q\nu\lambda + 2r\lambda\mu;$$

then at A we have $\mu = 0$ and $\nu = 0$, so that P is then the value of Σ; similarly Q and R are the values of Σ at B and C respectively. But by Art. 177 we have the same value for Σ whatever be the position of T; thus

$$P = P(\lambda^2 + \mu^2 + \nu^2) + 2p\mu\nu + 2q\nu\lambda + 2r\lambda\mu;$$

therefore $0 = 2p\mu\nu + 2q\nu\lambda + 2r\lambda\mu.$

This holds then for every position of T. Suppose T is at *any point* of the great circle of which A is the pole; then $\lambda = 0$: thus *we get* $p\mu\nu = 0$, and therefore $p = 0$. Similarly $q = 0$, and $r = 0$.

179. Let there be any number of fixed points on the surface of a sphere; denote them by $H_1, H_2, H_3, \dots$; from any two points T and U on the surface of the sphere arcs are drawn to the fixed points: it is required to find the sum of the products of the corresponding cosines, that is

$$\cos TH_1 \cos UH_1 + \cos TH_2 \cos UH_2 + \cos TH_3 \cos UH_3 + \dots.$$

Let the notation be the same as in Art. 174; and let $\lambda'\,\mu'\,\nu'$ be the cosines of the arcs which join U with A, B, C respectively. Then by Art. 166,

$$\cos TH_1 \cos UH_1 = \left(\lambda l_1 + \mu m_1 + \nu n_1\right)\left(\lambda' l_1 + \mu' m_1 + \nu' n_1\right) =$$

$$\lambda\lambda' l_1^2 + \mu\mu' m_1^2 + \nu\nu' n_1^2 + \left(\lambda\mu' + \mu\lambda'\right) l_1 m_1 + \left(\mu\nu' + \nu\mu'\right) m_1 n_1$$
$$+ \left(\nu\lambda' + \lambda\nu'\right) n_1 l_1.$$

Similar results hold for $\cos TH_2 \cos UH_2$, $\cos TH_3 \cos UH_3$,... Hence, with the notation of Art. 174, the required sum is

$$\lambda\lambda' P + \mu\mu' Q + \nu\nu' R + \left(\mu\nu' + \nu\mu'\right) p + \left(\nu\lambda' + \lambda\nu'\right)$$
$$q + \left(\lambda\mu' + \mu\lambda'\right) r.$$

Now by properly choosing the position of the triangle ABC we have p, q, and r each zero as in Art. 174; and thus the required sum becomes

$$\lambda\lambda' P + \mu\mu' Q + \nu\nu' R.$$

180. The result obtained in Art. 174 may be considered as a particular case of that just given; namely the case in which the points T and U coincide.

181. A sphere is described about a regular polyhedron; from any two points on the surface of the sphere arcs are drawn to the solid angles of the polyhedron: it is required to find the sum of the products of the corresponding cosines.

With the notation of Art. 179 we see that the sum is

$$\lambda\lambda' P + \mu\mu' Q + \nu\nu' R.$$

And here $P = Q = R = \dfrac{S}{3}$, by Art. 177.

Thus the sum $= \dfrac{S}{3}(\lambda\lambda' + \mu\mu' + \nu\nu') = \dfrac{S}{3}\cos TU$.

Thus the sum of the products of the cosines is equal to the product of the cosine TU into a third of the number of the solid angles of the regular polyhedron.

182. The result obtained in Art. 177 may be considered as a particular case of that just given; namely, the case in which the points *T* and *U* coincide.

183. If *TU* is a quadrant then cos *TU* is zero, and the sum of the products of the cosines in Art. 181 is zero. The results $p = 0$, $q = 0$, $r = 0$, are easily seen to be all special examples of this particular case.

MISCELLANEOUS PROPOSITIONS

184. *To find the locus of the vertex of a spherical triangle of given base and area.*

Let AB be the given base, $= c$ suppose, $AC = \theta$, $BAC = \phi$. Since the area is given the spherical excess is known; denote it by E; then by Art. 103,

$$\cot \frac{1}{2} E = \cot \frac{1}{2} \theta \cot \frac{1}{2} c \operatorname{cosec} \phi + \cot \phi;$$

therefore $\quad \sin\left(\phi - \frac{1}{2} E\right) = \cot \frac{1}{2} \theta \cot \frac{1}{2} c \sin \frac{1}{2} E;$

therefore $\quad 2 \cot \frac{1}{2} c \sin \frac{1}{2} E \cos^2 \frac{\theta}{2} = \sin \theta \sin\left(\phi - \frac{1}{2} E\right);$

therefore

$$\cos \theta \cot \frac{1}{2} c \sin \frac{1}{2} E + \sin \theta \cos\left(\phi - \frac{1}{2} E + \frac{\pi}{2}\right) = -\cot \frac{1}{2} c \sin \frac{1}{2} E.$$

Comparing this with equation (1) of Art. 133, we see that the required locus is a circle. If we call α, β the angular co-ordinates of its pole, we have

$$\tan \alpha = \frac{1}{\cot \frac{1}{2} c \sin \frac{1}{2} E} = \frac{\tan \frac{1}{2} c}{\sin \frac{1}{2} E}.$$

$$\beta = \frac{1}{2} E - \frac{\pi}{2}.$$

It may be presumed from symmetry that the pole of this circle is in the great circle which bisects AB at right angles; and this presumption is easily verified.

For the equation to that great circle is

$$0 = \cos \theta \cos \left(\frac{\pi}{2} - \frac{c}{2} \right) + \sin \theta \sin \left(\frac{\pi}{2} - \frac{c}{2} \right) \cos(\phi - \pi)$$

and the values $\theta = \alpha$, $\phi = \beta$ satisfy this equation.

185. *To find the angular distance between the poles of the inscribed and circumscribed circles of a triangle.*

Let P denote the pole of the inscribed circle, and Q the pole of the circumscribed circle of a triangle ABC; then $PAB = \frac{1}{2} A$, by Art.89, and $QAB = S - C$, by Art. 92; hence

$$\cos PAQ = \cos \frac{1}{2}(B - C);$$

and $\cos PQ = \cos PA \cos QA + \sin PA \sin QA \cos \dfrac{1}{2}(B - C).$

Now, by Art. 62 (see the figure of Art. 89),

$$\cos PA = \cos PE \cos AE = \cos r \cos(s - a),$$

$$\sin PA = \frac{\sin PE}{\sin PAE} = \frac{\sin r}{\sin \frac{1}{2}A};$$

thus

$$\cos PQ = \cos R \cos r \cos(s - a) + \sin R \sin r$$
$$\cos \frac{1}{2}(B - C)\operatorname{cosec}\frac{1}{2}A.$$

Therefore, by Art. 54

$$\cos PQ = \cos R \cos r \cos(s - a) + \sin R \sin r \sin \frac{1}{2}$$
$$(b + c)\operatorname{cosec}\frac{1}{2}a,$$

therefore

$$\frac{\cos PQ}{\cos R \sin r} = \cot r \cos(s - a) + \tan R \sin \frac{1}{2}(b + c)\operatorname{cosec}\frac{1}{2}a.$$

Now $\cot r = \dfrac{\sin s}{n}, \tan R = \dfrac{2\sin\frac{1}{2}a\sin\frac{1}{2}b\sin\frac{1}{2}c}{n},$

therefore

$$\frac{\cos PQ}{\cos R \sin r} = \frac{1}{n}\left\{ \sin s \cos(s-a) + 2\sin\frac{1}{2}(b+c)\sin\frac{1}{2}b\sin\frac{1}{2}c \right\}$$

$$= \frac{1}{2n}(\sin a + \sin b + \sin c).$$

Hence

$$\left(\frac{\cos PQ}{\cos R \sin r} \right)^2 - 1 = \frac{1}{4n^2}(\sin a + \sin b + \sin c)^2 - 1$$

$$= (\cot r + \tan R)^2 \text{ (by Art. 94)};$$

therefore $\cos^2 PQ = \cos^2 R \sin^2 r + \cos^2(R-r)$,

$$\sin^2 PQ = \sin^2(R-r) - \cos^2 R \sin^2 r.$$

186. *To find the angular distance between the pole of the circumscribed circle and the pole of one of the escribed circles of a triangle.*

Let Q denote the pole of the circumscribed circle, and Q_1 the pole of the escribed circle opposite to the angle A. Then it may be shewn that $QBQ_1 = \frac{1}{2}\pi + \frac{1}{2}(C-A)$, and

$$\cos QQ_1 = \cos R \cos r_1 \cos(s-c) - \sin R \sin r_1$$

$$\sin\frac{1}{2}(C-A)\sec\frac{1}{2}B$$

$$= \cos R \cos r_1 \cos(s-c) - \sin R \sin r_1$$

$$\sin\frac{1}{2}(c-a)\operatorname{cosec}\frac{1}{2}b.$$

Therefore

$$\frac{\cos QQ_1}{\sin r_1 \cos R} = \cot r_1 \cos(s-c) - \tan R \sin\frac{1}{2}(c-a)\operatorname{cosec}\frac{1}{2}b;$$

by reducing as in the preceding Article, the right-hand member of the last equation becomes

$$\frac{1}{2n}(\sin b + \sin c - \sin a);$$

hence $\left(\dfrac{\cos QQ_1}{\cos R \sin r_1}\right)^2 - 1 = (\tan R - \cot r_1)^2, (\text{Art.}94);$

therefore $\cos^2 QQ_1 = \cos^2 R \sin^2 r_1 + \cos^2(R+r_1),$

and $\sin^2 QQ_1 = \sin^2(R+r_1) - \cos^2 R \sin^2 r_1.$

187. *The arc which passes through the middle points of the sides of any triangle upon a given base will meet the base produced at a fixed point, the distance of which from the middle point of the base is a quadrant.*

Let ABC be any triangle, E the middle point of AC, and F the middle point of AB; let the arc which joins E and F when produced meet BC produced at Q. Then

$$\frac{\sin BQ}{\sin BF} = \frac{\sin BFQ}{\sin BQF}, \frac{\sin AQ}{\sin AF} = \frac{\sin AFQ}{\sin AQF};$$

therefore $\dfrac{\sin BQ}{\sin AQ} = \dfrac{\sin AQF}{\sin BQF},$

similarly
$$\frac{\sin CQ}{\sin AQ} = \frac{\sin AQF}{\sin CQF};$$

therefore $\sin BQ = \sin CQ$; therefore $BQ + CQ = \pi$.

Hence if D be the middle point of BC

$$DQ = \frac{1}{2}(BQ + CQ) = \frac{1}{2}\pi.$$

188. *If three arcs be drawn from the angles of a spherical triangle through any point to meet the opposite sides, the products of the sines of the alternate segments of the sides are equal.*

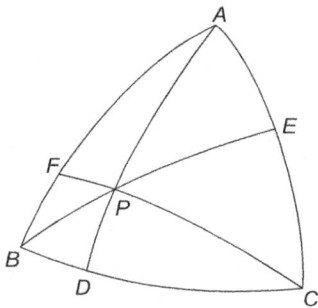

Let P be any point, and let arcs be drawn from the angles A, B, C passing through P and meeting the opposite sides at D, E, F. Then

$$\frac{\sin BD}{\sin BP} = \frac{\sin BPD}{\sin BDP}, \qquad \frac{\sin CD}{\sin CP} = \frac{\sin CPD}{\sin CDP},$$

therefore
$$\frac{\sin BD}{\sin CD} = \frac{\sin BPD}{\sin CPD}\frac{\sin BP}{\sin CP}.$$

Similar expressions may be found for $\dfrac{\sin CE}{\sin AE}$ and $\dfrac{\sin AF}{\sin BF}$; and hence it follows obviously that

$$\frac{\sin BD}{\sin CD}\frac{\sin CE}{\sin AE}\frac{\sin AF}{\sin BF} = 1;$$

therefore $\sin BD \sin CE \sin AF = \sin CD \sin AE \sin BF$.

189. Conversely, when the points D, E, F in the sides of a spherical triangle are such that the relation given in the preceding Article holds, the arcs which join these points with the opposite angles respectively *pass through a common point*. Hence the following propositions may be established: the perpendiculars from the angles of a spherical triangle on the opposite sides meet at a point; the arcs which bisect the angles of a spherical triangle meet at a point; the arcs which join the angles of a spherical triangle with the middle points of the opposite sides meet at a point; the arcs which join the angles of a spherical triangle with the points where the inscribed circle touches the opposite sides respectively meet at a point.

Another mode of establishing such propositions has been exemplified in Arts. 139 and 140.

190. *If AB and A'B' be any two equal arcs AA' and AA' and BB' be bisected at right angles by arcs meeting at P, then AB and A'B' subtend equal angles at P.*

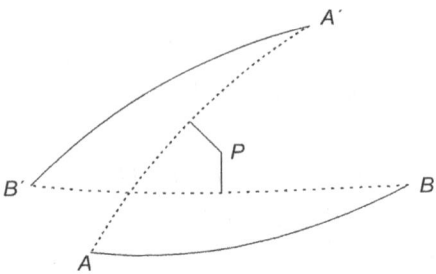

For $PA = PA'$ and $PB = PB'$; hence the sides of the triangle PAB are respectively equal to those of $PA'B'$; therefore the angle APB = the angle $A'PB'$.

This simple proposition has an important application to the motion of a rigid body of which one point is fixed. For conceive a sphere capable of motion round its centre which is fixed; then it appears from this proposition that any two fixed points on the sphere, as A and B, can be brought into any other positions, as A' and B', by rotation round an axis passing through the centre of the sphere and a certain point P. Hence it may be inferred that any change of position in a rigid body, of which one point is fixed, may be effected by rotation round some axis through the fixed point.

(De Morgan's *Differential and Integral Calculus*, page 489.)

191. Let P denote any point within any *plane* angle AOB, and from P draw perpendiculars on the straight lines OA and OB; then it is evident that these perpendiculars include an angle which is the *supplement* of the angle AOB. The corresponding fact with respect to a *solid* angle is worthy of notice. Let there be a solid angle formed by three plane

angles, meeting at a point *O*. From any point *P* within the solid angle, draw perpendiculars *PL, PM, PN* on the three planes which form the solid angle; then the spherical triangle which corresponds to the three planes *LPM, MPN, NPL* is the *polar triangle* of the spherical triangle which corresponds to the solid angle at *O*. This remark is due to Professor De Morgan.

192. Suppose three straight lines to meet at a point and form a solid angle; let α, β, and γ denote the angles contained by these three straight lines taken in pairs: then it has been proposed to call the expression $\sqrt{(1 - \cos^2 \alpha - \cos^2 \beta - \cos^2 \gamma + 2 \cos \alpha \cos \beta \cos \gamma)}$, the *sine of the solid angle*. See Baltzer's *Theorie. . . der Determinanten*, 2nd edition, page 177. Adopting this definition it is easy to shew that the sine of a solid angle lies between zero and unity.

We know that the area of a plane triangle is half the product of two sides into the sine of the included angle: by Art. 156 we have the following analogous proposition; the volume of a tetrahedron is one sixth of the product of three edges into the sine of the solid angle which they form.

Again, we know in mechanics that if three forces acting at a point are in equilibrium, each force is as the sine of the angle between the directions of the other two: the following proposition is analogous; if four forces acting at a point are in equilibrium each force is as the sine of the solid angle formed by the directions of the other three. See *Statics*, Chapter 2.

193. Let a sphere be described about a regular polyhedron; let perpendiculars be drawn from the centre of the sphere on the faces of the polyhedron, and produced to meet the surface of the sphere: then it is obvious from symmetry that the points of intersection must be the angular points of another regular polyhedron.

This may be verified. It will be found on examination that if S be the number of solid angles, and F the number of faces of one regular polyhedron, then another regular polyhedron exists which has S faces and F solid angles. See Art. 151.

194. *Polyhedrons.* The result in Art. 150 was first obtained by Euler; the demonstration which is there given is due to Legendre. The demonstration shews that the result is true in many cases in which the polyhedron has re-entrant solid angles; for all that is necessary for the demonstration is, that it shall be possible to take a point within the polyhedron as the centre of a sphere, so that the polygons, formed as in Art. 150, shall not have any coincident portions. The result, however, is generally true, even in cases in which the condition required by the demonstration of Art. 150 is not satisfied. We shall accordingly give another demonstration, and shall then deduce some important consequences from the result. We begin with a theorem which is due to Cauchy.

195. *Let there be any network of rectilineal figures, not necessarily in one plane, but not forming a closed surface; let E be the number of edges, F the number of figures, and S the number of corner points: then F + S = E + 1.*

This theorem is obviously true in the case of a single plane figure; for then $F = 1$, and $S = E$. It can be shewn to be generally true by induction. For assume the theorem to be true for a network of F figures; and suppose that a rectilineal figure of n sides is added to this network, so that the network and the additional figure have m sides coincident, and therefore $m + 1$ corner points coincident. And with respect to the new network which is thus formed, let E', F', S' denote the same things as E, F, S with respect to the old network. Then

$$E' = E + n - m, \quad F' = F + 1, \quad S' = S + n - (m + 1);$$

therefore $\quad F' + S' - E' = F + S - E$.

But $F + S = E + 1$, by hypothesis; therefore $F' + S' = E' + 1$.

196. To demonstrate Euler's theorem we suppose one face of a polyhedron removed, and we thus obtain a network of rectilineal figures to which Cauchy's theorem is applicable. Thus

$$F - 1 + S = E + 1;$$

therefore $\quad\quad F + S = E + 2.$

197. *In any polyhedron the number of faces with an odd number of sides is even, and the number of solid angles formed with an odd number of plane angles is even.*

Let a, b, c, d, ... denote respectively the numbers of faces which are triangles, quadrilaterals, pentagons, hexagons,... Let α, β, γ, δ,... denote respectively the numbers of the solid angles which are formed with three, four, five, six,... plane angles.

Then, each edge belongs to two faces, and terminates at *two* solid angles; therefore

$$2E = 3a + 4b + 5c + 6d + \ldots,$$

$$2E = 3\alpha + 4\beta + 5\gamma + 6\delta + \ldots,$$

From these relations it follows that $a + c + e + \ldots$, and $\alpha + \gamma + \varepsilon + \ldots$ are *even* numbers.

198. With the notation of the preceding Article we have

$$F = a + b + c + d + \ldots,$$

$$S = \alpha + \beta + \gamma + \delta + \ldots$$

From these combined with the former relations we obtain

$$2E - 3F = b + 2c + 3d + \ldots,$$

$$2E - 3S = \beta + 2\gamma + 3\delta + \ldots,$$

Thus $2E$ cannot be less than $3F$, or less than $3S$.

199. From the expressions for E, F, and S, given in the two preceding Articles, combined with the result $2F + 2S = 4 + 2E$, we obtain

$$2(a+b+c+d+\ldots) + 2(\alpha+\beta+\gamma+\delta+\ldots)$$
$$= 4 + 3a + 4b + 5c + 6d + \ldots,$$
$$2(a+b+c+d+\ldots) + 2(\alpha+\beta+\gamma+\delta+\ldots)$$
$$= 4 + 3\alpha + 4\beta + 5\gamma + 6\delta + \ldots,$$

therefore

$$2(\alpha + \beta + \gamma + \delta + \ldots) - (a + 2b + 3c + 4d + \ldots) = 4, \quad (1)$$

$$2(a+b+c+d+...) - (\alpha + 2\beta + 3\gamma + 4\delta + ...) = 4 \qquad (2)$$

Therefore, by addition

$$a + \alpha - (c + \gamma) - 2(d + \delta) - 3(e + \varepsilon) - ...... = 8.$$

Thus the number of triangular faces together with the number of solid angles formed with three plane angles cannot be less than eight.

Again, from (1) and (2), by eliminating α, we obtain

$$3a + 2b + c - e - 2f - ... - 2\beta - 4\gamma - ... = 12,$$

so that $3a + 2b + c$ cannot be less than 12. From this result various inferences can be drawn; thus for example, *a solid cannot be formed which shall have no triangular, quadrilateral, or pentagonal faces.*

In like manner, we can shew that $3\alpha + 2\beta + \gamma$ cannot be less than 12.

200. Poinsot has shewn that in addition to the five well-known *regular polyhedrons*, four other solids exist which are perfectly symmetrical in shape, and which might therefore also be called *regular*. We may give an idea of the nature of Poinsot's results by referring to the case of a polygon. Suppose five points A, B, C, D, E, placed in succession at equal distances round the circumference of a circle. If we draw a straight line from each point to the next point, we form an ordinary regular pentagon. Suppose however we join the points by straight lines in the following order, A to C,

C to *E*, *E* to *B*, *B* to *D*, *D* to *A*; we thus form a star-shaped symmetrical figure, which might be considered a regular pentagon.

It appears that, in a like manner, four, and only four, new regular solids can be formed. To such solids, the faces of which intersect and cross, Euler's theorem does not apply.

201. Let us return to Art. 195, and suppose *e* the number of edges *in* the bounding contour, and *e'* the number of edges *within* it; also suppose *s* the number of corners in the bounding contour, and *s'* the number *within* it. Then

$$E = e + e'; \ S = s + s';$$

therefore $\quad 1 + e + e' = s + s' + F.$

But $\qquad\qquad\quad e = s;$

therefore $\quad 1 + e' = s' + F.$

We can now demonstrate an extension of Euler's theorem, which has been given by Cauchy.

202. *Let a polyhedron be decomposed into any number of polyhedrons at pleasure; let P be the number thus formed, S the number of solid angles, F the number of faces, E the number of edges: then $S + F = E + P + 1$.*

For suppose all the polyhedrons united, by starting with one and adding one at a time. Let *e*, *f*, *s* be respectively the numbers of edges, faces, and solid angles in the first; let *e'*, *f'*, *s'* be respectively the numbers of edges, faces, and solid angles in the second which are not common to it and the first; let e'', f'', s'' be respectively the numbers of edges, faces, and solid angles in the third which are not common to it and the first or second; and so on. Then we have the following results, namely, the first by Art. 196, and the others by Art. 201;

$$s + f = e + 2,$$

$$s' + f' = e' + 1,$$

$$s'' + f'' = e'' + 1,$$

$$\dots\dots\dots\dots\dots\dots$$

By addition, since $s + s' + s'' + \dots = S$, $f + f' + f'' + \dots = F$, and $e + e' + e'' + \dots = E$, we obtain

$$S + F = E + P + 1.$$

203. The following references will be useful to those who study the theory of polyhedrons. Euler, *Novi Commentarii Academiæ... Petropolitanæ*, Vol. IV. 1758; Legendre, *G'eom'etrie*; Poinsot, *Journal de l' Ecole Polytechnique*, Cahier X; Cauchy, *Journal de l' Ecole Polytechnique*, Cahier XVI; Poinsot and Bertrand, *Comptes Rendus... de l'Academie des Sciences*, Vol. XLVI; Catalan, *Theoremes et Problemes de Geometrie Elementaire*; Kirkman, *Philosophical Transactions* for 1856 and subsequent years; Listing, *Abhandlungen der Koniglichen Gesellschaft... zu Gottingen*, Vol. X.

MISCELLANEOUS EXAMPLES

1.   Find the locus of the vertices of all right-angled spherical triangles having the same hypotenuse; and from the equation obtained, prove that the locus is a circle when the radius of the sphere is infinite.

2. AB is an arc of a great circle on the surface of a sphere, C its middle point: shew that the locus of the point P, such that the angle APC = the angle BPC, consists of two great circles at right angles to one another. Explain this when the triangle becomes plane.

3.   On a given arc of a sphere, spherical triangles of equal area are described: shew that the locus of the angular point opposite to the given arc is defined by the equation

$$\tan^{-1}\left\{\frac{\tan(\alpha+\phi)}{\sin\theta}\right\} + \tan^{-1}\left\{\frac{\tan(\alpha-\phi)}{\sin\theta}\right\}$$
$$+ \tan^{-1}\left\{\frac{\tan\theta}{\sin(\alpha+\phi)}\right\} + \tan^{-1}\left\{\frac{\tan\theta}{\sin(\alpha-\phi)}\right\} = \beta,$$

where 2α is the length of the given arc, θ the arc of the great circle drawn from any point P in the locus perpendicular to the given arc, ϕ the inclination of the great circle on which θ is measured to the great circle bisecting the given arc at right angles, and β a constant.

4.   In any spherical triangle

$$\tan c = \frac{\cot A \cot a + \cot B \cot b}{\cot a \cot b - \cos A \cos B}.$$

5. If θ, ϕ, ψ denote the distances from the angles A, B, C respectively of the point of intersection of arcs bisecting the angles of the spherical triangle ABC, shew that

$$\cos \theta \sin(b - c) + \cos \phi \sin(c - a) + \cos \psi \sin(a - b) = 0.$$

6. If A', B', C' be the poles of the sides BC, CA, AB of a spherical triangle ABC, shew that the great circles AA', BB', CC' meet at a point P, such that

$$\cos PA \cos BC = \cos PB \cos CA = \cos PC \cos AB.$$

7. If O be the point of intersection of arcs AD, BE, CF drawn from the angles of a triangle perpendicular to the opposite sides and meeting them at D, E, F respectively, shew that

$$\frac{\tan AD}{\tan OD}, \frac{\tan BE}{\tan OE}, \frac{\tan CF}{\tan OF}$$

are respectively equal to

$$1 + \frac{\cos A}{\cos B \cos C}, 1 + \frac{\cos B}{\cos A \cos C}, 1 + \frac{\cos C}{\cos A \cos B}.$$

8. If p, q, r be the arcs of great circles drawn from the angles of a triangle perpendicular to the opposite sides, (α, α'), (β, β'), (γ, γ') the segments into which these arcs are divided, shew that

$$\tan \alpha \tan \alpha' = \tan \beta \tan \beta' = \tan \gamma \tan \gamma';$$

and

$$\frac{\cos p}{\cos \alpha \cos \alpha'} = \frac{\cos q}{\cos \beta \cos \beta'} = \frac{\cos r}{\cos \gamma \cos \gamma'}.$$

9. In a spherical triangle if arcs be drawn from the angles to the middle points of the opposite sides, and if α, α' be the two parts of the one which bisects the side a, shew that

$$\frac{\sin \alpha}{\sin \alpha'} = 2\cos\frac{a}{2}.$$

10. The arc of a great circle bisecting the sides AB, AC of a spherical triangle cuts BC produced at Q: shew that

$$\cos AQ \sin\frac{a}{2} = \sin\frac{c-b}{2}\sin\frac{c+b}{2}.$$

11. If $ABCD$ be a spherical quadrilateral, and the opposite sides AB, CD when produced meet at E, and AD, BC meet at F, the ratio of the sines of the arcs drawn from E at right angles to the diagonals of the quadrilateral is the same as the ratio of those from F.

12. If $ABCD$ be a spherical quadrilateral whose sides AB, DC are produced to meet at P, and AD, BC at Q, and whose diagonals AC, BD intersect at R, then
$$\sin AB \sin CD \cos P = \sin AD \sin BC \cos Q$$
$$= \sin AC \sin BD \cos R.$$

13. If A' be the angle of the chordal triangle which corresponds to the angle A of a spherical triangle, shew that

$$\cos A' = \sin(S - A)\cos\frac{a}{2}.$$

14. If the tangent of the radius of the circle described about a spherical triangle is equal to twice the tangent of the radius of the circle inscribed in the triangle, the triangle is equilateral.

15. The arc AP of a circle of the same radius as the sphere is equal to the greater of two sides of a spherical triangle, and the arc AQ taken in the same direction is equal to the less; the sine PM of AP is divided at E, so that $\dfrac{EM}{PM}=$ the natural cosine of the angle included by the two sides, and EZ is drawn parallel to the tangent to the circle at Q. Shew that the remaining side of the spherical triangle is equal to the arc QPZ.

16. If through any point P within a spherical triangle ABC great circles be drawn from the angular points A, B, C to meet the opposite sides at a, b, c respectively, prove that

$$\frac{\sin Pa \cos PA}{\sin Aa}+\frac{\sin Pb \cos PB}{\sin Bb}+\frac{\sin Pc \cos PC}{\sin Cc}=1.$$

17. A and B are two places on the Earth's surface on the same side of the equator, A being further from the equator than B. If the bearing of A from B be more nearly due East than it is from any other place in the same latitude as B, find the bearing of B from A.

18. From the result given in example 18 of Chapter 5 infer the possibility of a regular dodecahedron.

19. A and B are fixed points on the surface of a sphere, and P is any point on the surface. If a and b are given constants, shew that a fixed point S can always be found, in AB or AB produced, such that

$$a \cos AP + b \cos BP = s \cos SP,$$

where s is a constant.

20. $A, B, C,...$ are fixed points on the surface of a sphere; $a, b, c,...$ are given constants. If P be a point on the surface of the sphere, such that

$$a \cos AP + b \cos BP + c \cos CP + ... = \text{constant},$$

shew that the locus of P is a circle.

NUMERICAL SOLUTION OF SPHERICAL TRIANGLES

204. We shall give in this Chapter examples of the numerical solution of Spherical Triangles.

We shall first take right-angled triangles, and then oblique-angled triangles.

Right-Angled Triangles

205. Given $a = 37°48'12''$, $b = 59°44'16''$, $C = 90°$. To find c we have

$$\cos c = \cos a \cos b,$$
$$L \cos 37°48'12'' = 9.8976927$$
$$L \cos 59°44'16'' = \underline{9.7023945}$$
$$L \cos c + 10 = \overline{19.6000872}$$
$$c = 66°32'6''.$$

To find A we have

$$\cot A = \cot a \sin b,$$
$$L \cot 37°48'12'' = 10.1102655$$
$$L \sin 59°44'16'' = \underline{9.9363770}$$
$$L \cot A + 10 = 20.0466425$$
$$A = 41°55'45''.$$

To find B we have

$$\cot B = \cot b \sin a,$$
$$L \cot 59°44'16'' = 9.7660175$$
$$L \sin 37°48'12'' = \underline{9.7874272}$$
$$L \cot B + 10 = 19.5534447$$
$$B = 70°19'15''.$$

206. Given $A = 55°32'45'', C = 90°, c = 98°14'24''.$

To find a we have

$$\sin a = \sin c \sin A,$$
$$L \sin 98°14'24'' = 9.9954932$$
$$L \sin 55°32'45'' = \underline{9.9162323}$$
$$L \sin a + 10 = 19.9117255$$
$$a = 54°41'35''.$$

To find B we have

$$\cot B = \cos c \tan A.$$

Here cos c *is negative*; and therefore cot B will be negative, and B greater than a right angle. The numerical value of cos c is the same as that of cos $81°45'36''$.

$$L\cos 81°45'36'' = 9.1563065$$
$$L\tan 55°32'45'' = \underline{10.1636102}$$
$$L\cot(180° - B) + 10 = 19.3199167$$
$$180° - B = 78°12'4''$$
$$B = 101°47'56''.$$

To find *b* we have

$$\tan b = \tan c \cos A.$$

Here tan *c* is *negative*; and therefore tan *b* will be negative and *b* greater than a quadrant.

$$L\tan 81°45'36'' = 10.8391867$$
$$L\cos 55°32'45'' = 9.7526221$$
$$L\tan(180° - b) + 10 = \overline{20.5918088}$$
$$180° - b = 75°38'32''$$
$$b = 104°21'28''.$$

207. Given $A = 46°15'25'', C = 90°, a = 42°18'45''.$

To find *c* we have

$$\sin c = \frac{\sin a}{\sin A},$$

$$L\sin c = 10 + L\sin a - L\sin A,$$
$$10 + L\sin 42°18'45'' = 19.8281272$$
$$L\sin 46°15'25'' = \underline{9.8588065}$$
$$L\sin c = 9.9693207$$
$$c = 68°42'59'' \text{ or } 111°17'1''.$$

To find b we have

$$\sin b = \tan a \cot A,$$
$$L \tan 42°18'45'' = 9.9591983$$
$$L \cot 46°15'25'' = 9.9809389$$
$$\overline{L \sin b + 10 = 19.9401372}$$
$$b = 60°36'10'' \text{ or } 119°23'50''.$$

To find B we have

$$\sin B = \frac{\cos A}{\cos a},$$
$$L \sin B = 10 + L \cos A - L \cos a,$$
$$10 + L \cos 46°15'25'' = 19.8397454$$
$$L \cos 42°18'45'' = 9.8689289$$
$$\overline{L \sin B = 9.9708165}$$
$$B = 69°13'47'' \text{ or } 110°46'13''.$$

Oblique-Angled Triangles

208. Given $a = 70°14'20'', b = 49°24'10'', c = 38°46'10'$.

We shall use the formula given in Art. 45,

$$\tan \frac{1}{2} A = \sqrt{\left\{ \frac{\sin(s-b)\sin(s-c)}{\sin s \sin(s-a)} \right\}}.$$

Here
$$s = 79°12'20''$$
$$s - a = 8°58',$$
$$s - b = 29°48'10'',$$
$$s - c = 40°26'10''.$$

$$L\sin 29°48'10'' = 9.6963704$$

$$L\sin 40°26'10'' = 9.8119768$$

$$\overline{19.5083472}$$

$$L\sin 79°12'20'' = 9.9922465$$

$$L\sin 8°58' = 9.1927342$$

$$\overline{19.1849807}$$

$$19.5083472$$

$$\underline{19.1849807}$$

$$2).3233665$$

$$L\tan\frac{1}{2}A - 10 = \ \ .1616832$$

$$\frac{1}{2}A = 55°25'38''$$

$$A = 110°51'16''.$$

Similarly to find *B*,

$$L\sin 8°58' = \ \ 9.1927342$$

$$L\sin 40°26'10'' = \ \ \underline{9.8119768}$$

$$19.0047110$$

$$L\sin 79°12'2'' = \ \ 9.9922465$$

$$L\sin 29°48'10'' = \ \ 9.6963704$$

$$\overline{19.6886169}$$

$$19.0047110$$

$$\underline{19.6886169}$$

$$2)\ \overline{1}.3160941$$

$$L \tan \frac{1}{2} B - 10 = \overline{1}.6580470$$

$$L \tan \frac{1}{2} B = 9.6580470$$

$$\frac{1}{2} B = 24° 28' 2''$$

$$B = 48° 56' 4''.$$

Similarly to find C,

$$L \sin 8°58' = 9.1927342$$
$$L \sin 29°48'10'' = 9.6963704$$
$$\overline{18.8891046}$$
$$L \sin 79°12'20'' = 9.9922465$$
$$L \sin 40°26'10'' = 9.8119768$$
$$\overline{19.8042233}$$
$$18.8891046$$
$$19.8042233$$
$$\overline{2)\overline{1}.0848813}$$

$$L \tan \frac{1}{2} C - 10 = \overline{1}.5424406$$

$$L \tan \frac{1}{2} C = 9.5424406$$

$$\frac{1}{2} C = 19° 13' 24''$$

$$C = 38° 26' 48''.$$

209. Given $a = 68° 20'25''$, $b = 52°18'15''$, $C = 117°12'20''$.

By Art. 82,

$$\tan\frac{1}{2}(A+B) = \frac{\cos\frac{1}{2}(a-b)}{\cos\frac{1}{2}(a+b)}\cot\frac{1}{2}C,$$

$$\tan\frac{1}{2}(A-B) = \frac{\sin\frac{1}{2}(a-b)}{\sin\frac{1}{2}(a+b)}\cot\frac{1}{2}C.$$

$$\frac{1}{2}(a-b) = 8°1'5'', \frac{1}{2}(a+b) = 60°19'20'', \frac{1}{2}C = 58°36'10''.$$

$$L\cos 8°1'\ 5'' = 9.9957335$$
$$L\cot 58°36'10'' = 9.7855690$$
$$\overline{19.7813025}$$
$$L\cos 60°19'20'' = 9.6947120$$
$$L\tan\frac{1}{2}(A+B) = \overline{10.0865905}$$

$$\frac{1}{2}(A+B) = 50°40'28''$$

$$L\sin 8°\ 1'\ 5'' =\ 9.1445280$$
$$L\cot 58°36'10'' =\ 9.7855690$$
$$\overline{18.9300970}$$
$$L\sin 60°19'\ 20'' =\ 9.9389316$$

$$L\tan\frac{1}{2}(A-B) = 8.9911654$$

$$\frac{1}{2}(A-B) = 5°35'47''.$$

Therefore $A = 56°\ 16'15'', B = 45°4'41''.$

If we proceed to find c from the formula

$$\sin c = \frac{\sin a \sin C}{\sin A},$$

since $\sin C$ is greater than $\sin A$ we shall obtain two values for c both greater than a, and we shall not know which is the value to be taken.

We shall therefore determine c from formula (1) of Art. 54, which is free from ambiguity,

$$\cos \frac{1}{2}c = \frac{\cos \frac{1}{2}(a+b)\sin \frac{1}{2}C}{\cos \frac{1}{2}(A+B)},$$

$$L \cos 60°19'20'' = 9.6947120$$
$$L \sin 58°36'10'' = 9.9312422$$
$$\overline{ 19.6259542}$$
$$L \cos 50°40'28'' = 9.8019015$$
$$L \cos \frac{1}{2}c = \overline{ 9.8240527}$$
$$\frac{1}{2}c = 48°10'22''$$
$$c = 96°20'44''.$$

Or we may adopt the second method of Art. 82. First, we determine θ from the formula $\tan \theta = \tan b \cos C$.

Here $\cos C$ *is negative*, and therefore $\tan \theta$ will be negative, and θ greater than a right angle. The numerical value of $\cos C$ is the same as that of $\cos 62°47'40''$.

$$L\tan 52°18'15'' = 10.1119488$$
$$L\cos 62°47'40'' = 9.6600912$$
$$L\tan(180° - \theta) + 10 = \overline{19.7720400}$$
$$180° - \theta = 30°36'33''$$
$$\text{therefore}\,\theta = 149°23'27''.$$

Next, we determine *c* from the formula

$$\cos c = \frac{\cos b \cos(a - \theta)}{\cos \theta}.$$

Here cos θ *is negative*, and therefore cos *c* will be negative, and *c* will be greater than a right angle. The numerical value of cos θ is the same as that of cos(180° − θ), that is, of cos 30°36′33″; and the value of cos(*a* − θ) is the same as that of cos(θ − *a*), that is, of cos 81°3′2″.

$$L\cos 52°18'15'' = 9.7863748$$
$$L\cos 81°3'2'' = 9.1919060$$
$$\overline{18.9782808}$$
$$L\cos 30°36'33'' = \underline{9.9348319}$$
$$L\cos(180° - c) = 9.0434489$$
$$180° - c = 83°39'17''$$
$$c = 96°20'43''.$$

Thus by taking only the nearest number of seconds in the tables the two methods give values of *c* which differ by 1″; if, however, we estimate fractions of a second both methods will agree in giving about $43\frac{1}{2}$ as the number of seconds.

210. Given $a = 50°45'20''$, $b = 69°12'40''$, $A = 44°22'10''$.

By Art. 84, $\sin B = \dfrac{\sin b}{\sin a} \sin A,$

$L \sin 69°12'40'' = 9.9707626$

$L \sin 44°22'10'' = 9.8446525$

$\overline{ 19.8154151}$

$L \sin 50°45'20'' = 9.8889956$

$L \sin B = \overline{9.9264195}$

$B = 57°34'51''.4,$ or $122°25'8''.6.$

In this case there will be two solutions; see Art. 86. We will calculate C and c by Napier's analogies,

$$\tan \frac{1}{2}C = \frac{\cos \frac{1}{2}(b-a)}{\cos \frac{1}{2}(b+a)} \cot \frac{1}{2}(B+A),$$

$$\tan \frac{1}{2}c = \frac{\cos \frac{1}{2}(B+A)}{\cos \frac{1}{2}(B-A)} \tan \frac{1}{2}(b+a).$$

First take the smaller value of B; thus

$$\frac{1}{2}(B+A) = 50°58'30''.7, \frac{1}{2}(B-A) = 6°35'20''.7,$$

$$L \cos 9° 13' 40'' = 9.9943430$$

$$L \cot 50° 58' 30''.7 = 9.9087536$$

$$\overline{19.9030966}$$

$$L \cos 59° 59' = 9.6991887$$

$$L \tan \frac{1}{2} C = \overline{10.2039079}$$

$$\frac{1}{2} C = 57° 58' 55''.3$$

$$C = 115° 57' 50''.6.$$

$$L \cos 50° 58' 30''.7 = 9.7991039$$

$$L \tan 59° 59' = 10.2382689$$

$$\overline{20.0373728}$$

$$L \cos 6° 36' 20''.7 = 9.9971072$$

$$L \tan \frac{1}{2} c = \overline{10.0402656}$$

$$\frac{1}{2} c = 47° 39' 8''.2$$

$$c = 95° 18' 16''.4$$

Next take the larger value of B; thus

$$\frac{1}{2}(B + A) = 83° 23' 39''.3, \quad \frac{1}{2}(B - A) = 39° 1' 29''.3.$$

$$L\cos 9°\,13'\,40'' = 9.9943430$$

$$L\cot 83°\,23'\,39''.3 = 9.0637297$$

$$\overline{19.0580727}$$

$$L\cos 59°\,59' = 9.6991887$$

$$L\tan\frac{1}{2}C = \overline{9.3588840}$$

$$\frac{1}{2}C = 12°\,52'\,15''.8$$

$$C = 25°\,44'\,31''.6.$$

$$L\cos 83°\,23'\,39''.3 = 9.0608369$$

$$L\tan 59°\,59' = 10.2382689$$

$$\overline{19.2991058}$$

$$L\cos 39°\,1'\,29''.3 = 9.8903494$$

$$L\tan\frac{1}{2}c = \overline{9.4087564}$$

$$\frac{1}{2}c = 14°\,22'\,32''.6$$

$$c = 28°\,45'\,5''.2$$

The student can obtain more examples, which can be easily verified, from those here worked out, by interchanging the given and required quantities, or by making use of the polar triangle.

EXAMPLES

1. Given $b = 137°\,3'\,48''$, $A = 147°\,2'\,54''$, $C = 90°$.

    Results $c = 47°57'15'$, $a = 156°10'34''$, $B = 113°28'$.

2. Given $c = 61° 4' 56'$, $a = 40° 31' 20'$, $C = 90°$.

   Results $b = 50° 30' 29''$, $B = 61° 50' 28''$, $A = 47° 54' 21''$.

3. Given $A = 36°$, $B = 60°$, $C = 90°$.

   Results $a = 20° 54' 18''.5$, $b = 31° 43' 3'$, $c = 37° 21' 38''.5$.

4. Given $a = 59° 28' 27''$, $A = 66° 7' 20''$, $C = 90°$.

   Results $c = 70° 23' 42'$, $b = 48° 39' 16''$, $B = 52° 50' 20''$,

   or, $c = 109° 36' 18''$, $b = 131° 20' 44''$, $B = 127° 9' 40''$.

5. Given $c = 90°$, $a = 138° 4'$, $b = 109° 41'$.

   Results $C = 113° 28' 2''$, $A - 142° 11' 38''$, $B = 120° 15' 57''$.

6. Given $c = 90°$, $A = 131° 30'$, $B = 120° 32'$.

   Results $C = 109° 40' 20''$, $a = 127° 17' 51''$, $b = 113° 49' 31''$.

7. Given $a = 76° 35' 36''$, $b = 50° 10' 30''$, $c = 40° 0' 10''$.

   Results $A = 120° 36' 20''$, $B = 42° 15' 13''$, $C = 34° 15' 3''$.

8. Given $A = 129° 5' 28'$, $B = 142° 12' 42''$, $C = 105° 8' 10''$.

   Results $a = 135° 49' 20''$, $b = 144° 37' 15''$, $c = 60° 4' 54''$.

Made in the USA
Monee, IL
07 July 2026

56552344R00134